BERLIN

THE SECRET ATLAS

JONGLEZ PUBLISHING

THE AUTHORS

After earning his PhD in philosophy, **Tom Wolf** decided to dedicate himself to writing. He has written 22 crime novels, 3 guides inviting travelers to take a fresh look at the places they visit, and a guide on wines produced in the region of Brandenburg. After spending 12 years in Berlin-Mitte and Kreuzberg, he now lives in the north of the Berlin/Brandenburg metropolitan region where he looks after his vineyard and his small craft brewery. But that story is for another time ...

Manuel Roy had been a Germanophile for many years when he discovered Berlin like a punch in the face. He had seen Germany through the verses of Schiller and the paintings of Caspar David Friedrich, and found himself in a post-apocalyptic landscape full of punks scrupulously respectful of the selective sorting of rubbish. He admits to not having understood everything straight away. Twenty years of research later, with a doctorate in philosophy under his belt, having been a Berliner by adoption since 2000, and a guide in Berlin since 2013, Manuel now thinks that he has a better grasp of the city. But amazement is never far away. Despite its recent gentrification, the city never ceases to shake him up and surprise him. And it seems like he loves that.

We have taken great pleasure in drawing up *Berlin – The secret atlas* and hope that through its guidance you will, like us, continue to discover unusual, hidden or little-known aspects of the city. Descriptions of certain places are accompanied by thematic sections highlighting historical details or anecdotes as an aid to understanding the city in all its complexity. *Berlin – The secret atlas* also draws attention to the multitude of details found in places that we may pass every day without noticing. These are an invitation to look more closely at the urban landscape and, more generally, a means of seeing our own city with the curiosity and attention that we often display while travelling elsewhere ...

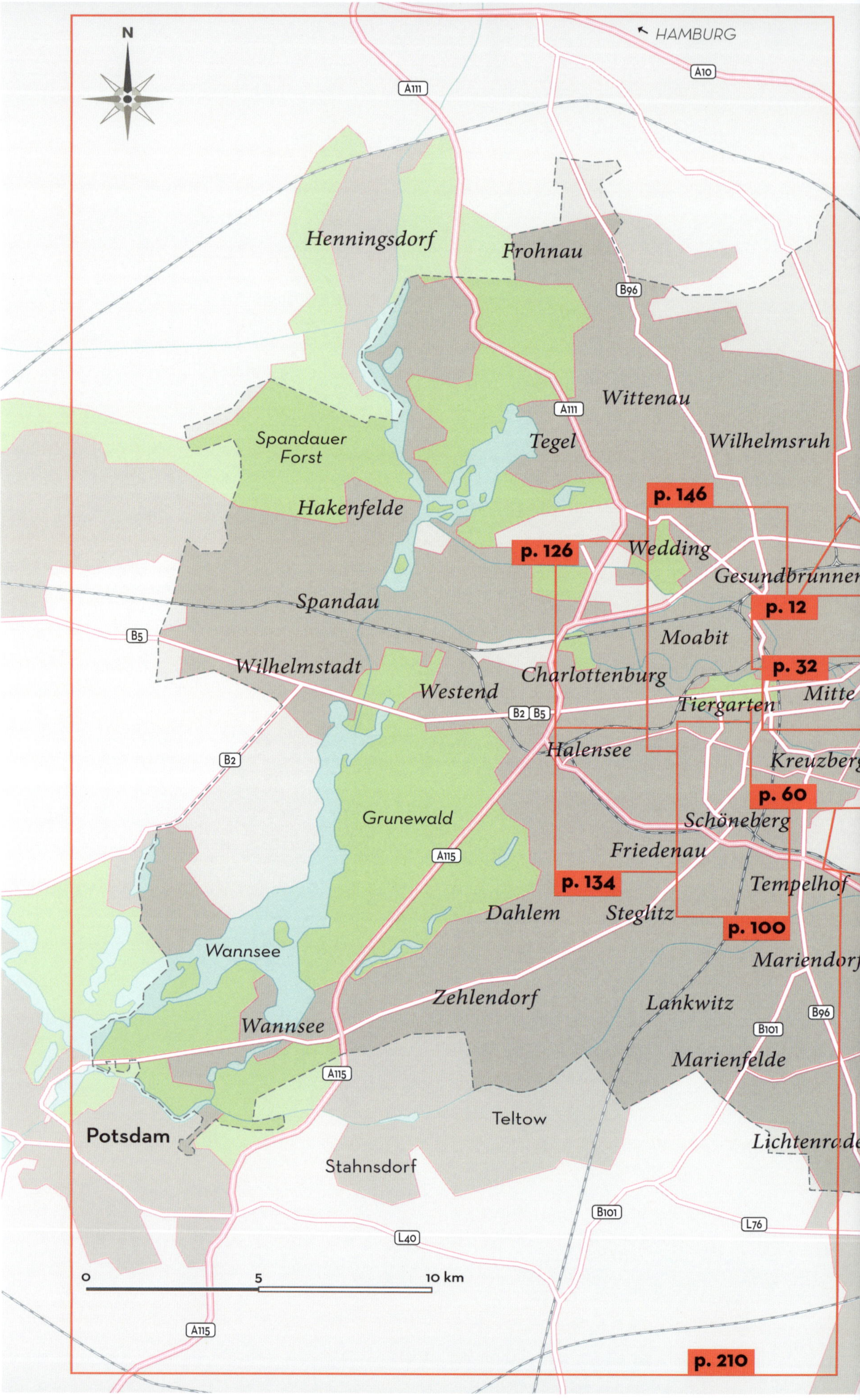
N
HAMBURG
A10
A111
Henningsdorf
Frohnau
B96
Wittenau
Tegel
Wilhelmsruh
Spandauer
Forst
Hakenfelde
p. 146
p. 126
Wedding
Gesundbrunnen
Spandau
p. 12
B5
Moabit
Wilhelmstadt
p. 32
Charlottenburg
Westend
Tiergarten
Mitte
B2 B5
Halensee
Kreuzberg
B2
p. 60
Grunewald
Schöneberg
A115
Friedenau
p. 134
Tempelhof
Dahlem
Steglitz
p. 100
Wannsee
Mariendorf
Zehlendorf
Lankwitz
B96
Wannsee
B101
Marienfelde
A115
Teltow
Potsdam
Lichtenrade
Stahnsdorf
B101
L76
L40
0
5
10 km
A115
p. 210

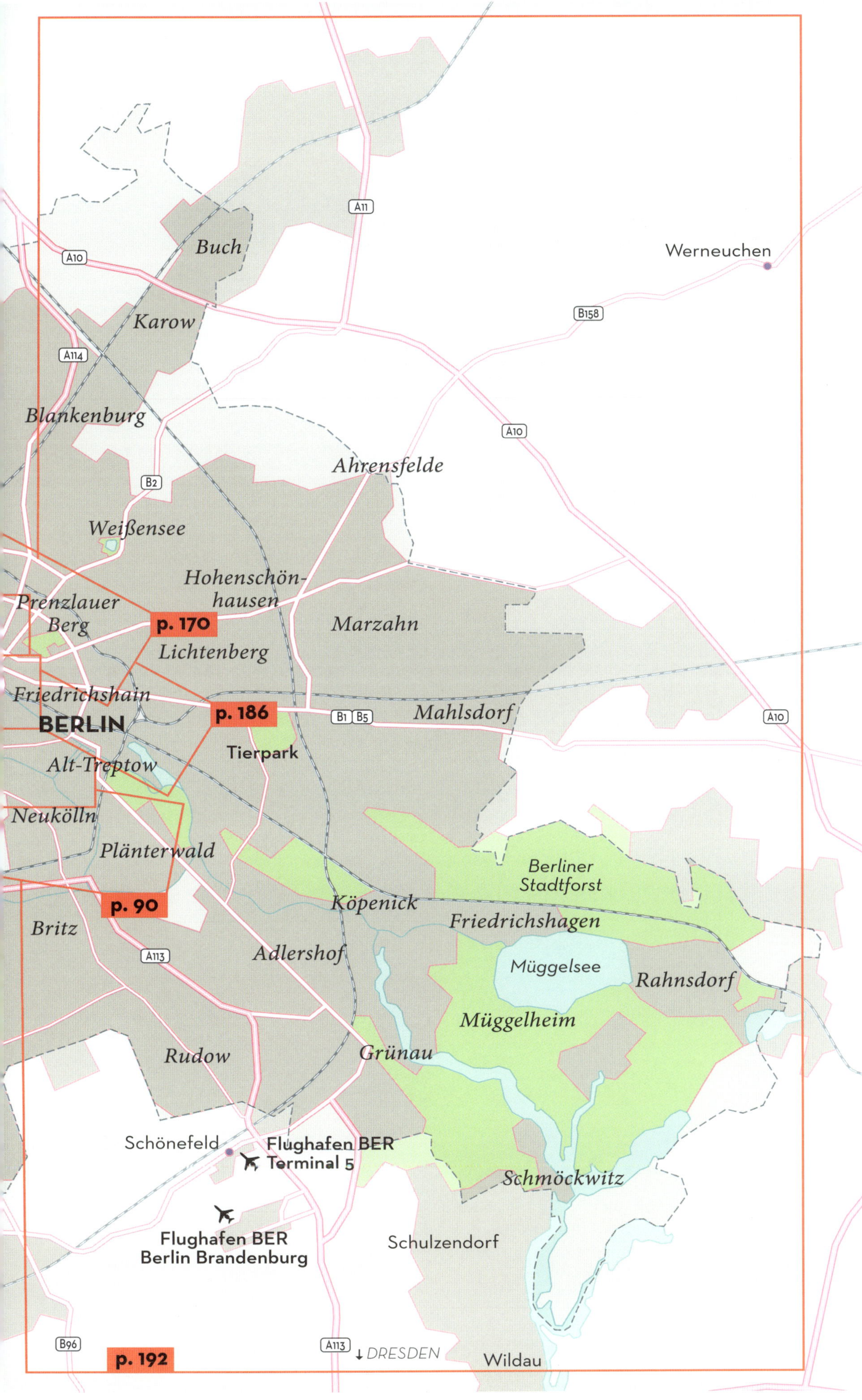
Buch
Karow
Blankenburg
Weißensee
Prenzlauer Berg
Hohenschönhausen
Lichtenberg
Friedrichshain
BERLIN
Alt-Treptow
Neukölln
Plänterwald
Britz
Ahrensfelde
Marzahn
Mahlsdorf
Tierpark
Köpenick
Adlershof
Rudow
Grünau
Berliner Stadtforst
Friedrichshagen
Müggelsee
Rahnsdorf
Müggelheim
Schmöckwitz
Schönefeld
Flughafen BER Terminal 5
Flughafen BER Berlin Brandenburg
Schulzendorf
Wildau
Werneuchen
↓ DRESDEN
A10
A11
A114
A113
B2
B158
B1
B5
B96
p. 170
p. 186
p. 90
p. 192

NORTH MITTE

SOUTH MITTE

KREUZBERG

NEUKÖLLN

SCHÖNEBERG

CHARLOTTENBURG

WILMERSDORF – FRIEDENAU

WEDDING – MOABIT – TIERGARTEN

PRENZLAUER BERG

FRIEDRICHSHAIN – RUMMELSBURG

PANKOW – LICHTENBERG – TREPTOW-KÖPENICK

SPANDAU – GRUNEWALD – STEGLITZ-ZEHLENDORF – SCHMARGENDORF – STAHNSDORF

NORTH MITTE

01. RABBIT SILHOUETTES ON CHAUSSEESTRAßE *p. 14*

02. THE WINDOWS OF THE INVALIDS' HOUSE *p. 16*

03. JAMES TURRELL'S INSTALLATION *p. 18*

04. ANIMAL ANATOMICAL THEATRE *p. 20*

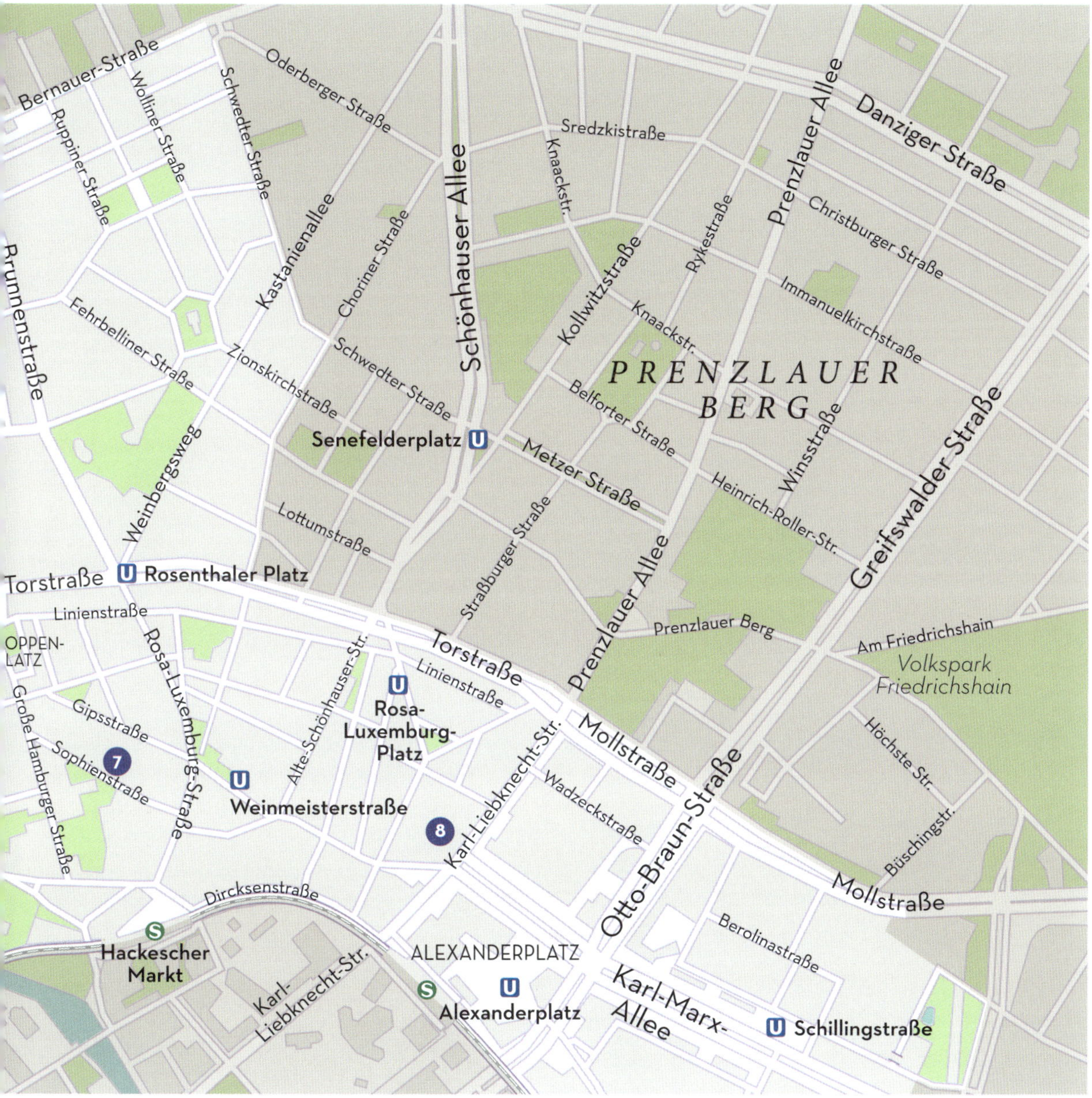
Bernauer-Straße
Wolliner-Straße
Ruppiner Straße
Schwedter Straße
Oderberger Straße
Kastanienallee
Choriner Straße
Schönhauser Allee
Sredzkistraße
Knaackstr.
Kollwitzstraße
Rykestraße
Prenzlauer Allee
Danziger Straße
Christburger Straße
Immanuelkirchstraße
Brunnenstraße
Fehrbelliner Straße
Zionskirchstraße
Schwedter Straße
Knaackstr.
PRENZLAUER BERG
Belforter Straße
Wörther Straße
Greifswalder Straße
Weinbergsweg
Senefelderplatz
Metzer Straße
Heinrich-Roller-Str.
Lottumstraße
Straßburger Straße
Torstraße
Rosenthaler Platz
Linienstraße
Rosa-Luxemburg-Straße
Alte-Schönhauser-Str.
Torstraße
Linienstraße
Prenzlauer Berg
Am Friedrichshain
Volkspark Friedrichshain
OPPEN-LATZ
Große Hamburger Straße
Gipsstraße
Sophienstraße
7
Rosa-Luxemburg-Platz
Weinmeisterstraße
Karl-Liebknecht-Str.
Mollstraße
Wadzeckstraße
Otto-Braun-Straße
Höchste Str.
Büschingstr.
8
Mollstraße
Dircksenstraße
Hackescher Markt
Karl-Liebknecht-Str.
ALEXANDERPLATZ
Alexanderplatz
Berolinastraße
Karl-Marx-Allee
Schillingstraße

01.

Chausseestraße 61
U6 (Schwartzkopffstraße)

RABBIT SILHOUETTES ON CHAUSSEESTRAßE

Crossing borders in fur coats

Despite all the security measures in place, the former border in the heart of Berlin was not impassable. Every day there were hundreds, even thousands, of crossings. These were not the rare and heroic crossings that occurred between 1961 and 1989, but rather the countless comings and goings of rabbits.

The demarcation between the former communist bloc and the West corresponds to a long green belt of great ecological value and rich biodiversity. During the Cold War, rabbits comfortably settled in these demarcated zones. With the end of the German Democratic Republic, everything became more complicated: cross-border infrastructures and so-called no man's lands disappeared faster than expected. The border areas were paradise: there were no hunters, nobody looking after their gardens, and no residents. For a long time, troops positioned at the borders had orders not to shoot the rabbits, and the rabbit tunnels heading towards West Germany were tolerated. It was only at the end of the German Democratic Republic that the rabbits became the victims of hunting rifles. Their population had grown to such proportions that there was a risk: by crossing the border unhindered, they could inspire men to do the same.

These days, rabbits are more likely to be spotted in one of the city's largest parks, such as Humboldthain or Tiergarten. But there is still one other place where some 120 rabbits roam around freely: the old border post between Wedding to the west and Mitte to the east.

By installing gleaming brass silhouettes of rabbits in the asphalt near number 61 Chausseestraße, artist Karla Sachse paid a special tribute in 1999 to these long-standing trans-border critters. There were initially many more of these little silhouettes, but rapid urbanisation (always a threat to art in public spaces) meant the brass rabbits ended up sharing the same fate as their organic cousins – in large cities, their numbers have also dwindled considerably, despite the ongoing efforts of the artist's friends.

02.

Scharnhorststraße 34-35
U6 (Naturkundemuseum)

THE WINDOWS OF THE INVALIDS' HOUSE

Windows for the war-wounded

Frederick II of Prussia, known as Frederick the Great, might have been a wiser tyrant than many other monarchs, but that did not stop him from going to war. When they weren't killed immediately on the battlefield or didn't die in horrendous agony like one soldier that Frederick II scolded and ordered to 'die with dignity', many of the king's soldiers came back wounded from the three wars he waged against Austria to reclaim Silesia, as well as the War of the Bavarian Succession.

During the 18th century, all those who came back crippled from these wars could not count on social welfare or unemployment benefits: Frederick the Great, therefore, built them a house where all their needs would be met, and in return they had to work to whatever extent they could.

The disabled soldiers made sure to keep this promise: a large part of the New Palace in Potsdam was actually built by them. The construction of the New Palace was meant to prove that, even after the third Silesian war (known throughout Europe as the Seven Years' War), Prussia had not been worn down. During the guided tour of the marble hall in the New Palace, you will notice a number of defects in the construction, such as evident cracks in the panelling, which are undoubtedly attributed to the disabled soldiers.

The Royal House of Invalids was inaugurated on 15 November 1748 in the presence of the king, who was warmly welcomed by the 631 veterans who had fought during the first two Silesian wars. Food and accommodation were provided to the boarders, who were also given clothing and attended by doctors. They could also pray to God in the chapel of their choice, Protestant or Catholic, and train to learn new trades, such as that of livestock breeder, brewer, or distiller in the various surrounding buildings. It was only later that they were requested to build the palace.

What about the soldiers who could no longer use their legs and were confined to the ancestor of today's wheelchair? In order to enable them to enjoy the view, windows overlooking the street and the courtyard were built close to floor level, as can still be seen today. According to the king, being able to look out onto what was still a bit of countryside on the doorstep of the city of Berlin had the power of 'regenerating the body and the mind'. For those who were unable to follow this programme, the remaining option was the nearby Invalids' Cemetery.

03.

Chapel at the Dorotheenstädtischer Cemetery I
Chausseestraße 126
U6 (Naturkundemuseum)

JAMES TURRELL'S INSTALLATION

Spectacular contemporary art in a cemetery

In the historic Dorotheenstadt Cemetery, the chapel near the main entrance is somewhat unique: since 2015, it has housed a contemporary artwork by American artist James Turrell, who is famous for his work with light.

Usually 30 minutes before nightfall, by reservation, visitors can enter the chapel, where a light installation is on display: shifting colors follow one another in harmony with the fading light of the late afternoon. The subtle effect immerses most visitors in a meditative atmosphere that is perfectly suited to the setting. Built in 1927–28, the chapel has no particular architectural significance but is ideally suited for J. Turrell's installation.

HERR GOTT DU BIST UNSERE ZUFLUCHT

04.

Philippstraße 12–13
U6 (Oranienburger Tor)

ANIMAL ANATOMICAL THEATRE

Elevator to the final act

Hidden away in the Charité, Berlin's university hospital, the animal anatomical theatre is an impressive building built in 1790 by Carl Gotthard Langhans, who found his inspiration in Andrea Palladio's Villa Rotonda in Italy. The bull skulls among the bas-reliefs over the outer windows hint at the building's purpose.

This type of theatre emerged across Europe to satisfy the growing interest in surgery and the human body. Berlin already had the anatomical theatre of the Collegium Medico-Chirurgicum, located since 1713 in the nearby Charité building complex. However, demonstrations performed on human bodies were not sufficient to meet the needs of the army: to the ruling class, animals used for military purposes – mainly horses and bulls – were just as important as soldiers. Therefore, in order for veterinarians to acquire the necessary knowledge, a second theatre dedicated to the dissection of animals was built.

Nowadays, Berlin's human anatomical theatre and the original building of the Charité complex no longer exist, but the building still referred to in German as 'TAT' gives an authentic idea of what these theatres were like. At the entrance, a small permanent exhibition details the history of the building and its architectural elements. Markings in the middle of the floor outline the area where the manually operated elevator hoisted the dead animals. And in addition to the particularly steep tiers of seats, the main attraction of the auditorium is its domed ceiling and the remarkable animal-themed grisaille paintings found there.

Since 2012, the Hermann von Helmholtz Center for Cultural Techniques (HKZ) uses the TAT as an innovative exhibition showroom and a centre for exchanges between scientific culture and the practice of exhibition making.

For more information about the theatres see the following double page spread.

In contrast to the many human anatomical theatres (there are eight in Germany alone), there were only half a dozen animal anatomical theatres across the whole of Europe.

ANATOMICAL THEATRES THROUGH HISTORY

An anatomical theatre (*Theatrum Anatomicum* in Latin) is a room dedicated to the teaching of human anatomy to medical students. The first ever amphitheatre was built in 1594 at the university of Padova (Italy), but Greek physician Herophilus of Chalcedon was already performing public dissections on human corpses at the Alexandria School of Medicine in Egypt in the year 300 BCE. These dissections were initially forbidden, then later authorised again during the Renaissance in western countries.

During the 15th century, dissections were performed in small improvised rooms, such as in the former hospital of the Royal Monastery of Santa María of Guadalupe (Spain), home to a prestigious medical school that trained famous surgeons and was granted a papal bull to perform *anathomías*, or dissections.

The discoveries of the great anatomist Vesalius (1514-1564) marked the beginning of a new era.

During the 16th century, anatomy became a very popular discipline not only among students, but also with the wider public. The first temporary anatomical theatres in Italy were based on a structure similar to that of amphitheatres of the Roman Empire. When dissections were abolished, the theatres were systematically destroyed. French anatomist Charles Estienne – known as Carolus Stephanus in Latin and Charles Stephens in English – later introduced a new architectural style in Paris, which remained very popular until the 19th century.

As the study of anatomy evolved, permanent anatomical theatres emerged. During the 16th and 17th centuries, two different design models came to the fore: those of the university of Padova and those of the university of Bologna. While both models incorporated wooden constructions within the largest building of their university, their architectural characteristics diverged.

In 1594 the first permanent anatomical theatre of the University of Padova was created by Girolamo Fabrici of Acquapendente; it took the form of a funnel (a truncated inverted cone) and could welcome up to 200 visitors. The theatre was in use for 278 years before being transformed into a museum. It became the reference model for a number of other amphitheatres: Leiden (Netherlands, 1597); Uppsala (Sweden, 1620); Copenhagen (Denmark, 1640); Groningen (Netherlands, 1654); Kiel (Germany, 1666); Amsterdam (Netherlands, 1691); Altdorf (Germany, 1650); Berlin (Germany, 1720); and Halle (Germany, 1727).

The other main architectural style for permanent amphitheatres followed that of the amphitheatre of Bologna, built in 1637 by the architect Antonio Paolucci. Rectangular in shape, like many medieval meeting places, it was decorated with magnificent wooden panels and sculptures depicting famous physicians of history. One anatomical theatre influenced by the Bologna model is the theatre of Ferrare (1731). During the 18th century, considerable modifications were made to the structure of anatomical buildings. The first autonomous anatomical theatre was built in Saint-Côme (France) by the Royal Academy of Surgery of Paris in 1694.

The academy later became the Ecole de Chirurgie (School of Surgery) and relocated to another building built by architect Jacques Gondoin. The design of the Grand Amphithéâtre (1768-1775) was influenced by the Pantheon in Rome, particularly apparent in its cul-de-four vault and demi-rose window. It could accommodate more than 1,400 visitors. In such a monumental environment, the corpse on the table and the professor performing the demonstration appeared almost in miniature. The school building was intended to evoke a sanctuary dedicated to Asclepius, the Greco-Roman god of medicine.

New methods for the preservation of human corpses required additional space to ensure the storage, preparation, maceration, investigation and exhibition of the corpses. All these requirements meant that the relevance of the traditional Theatrum Anatomicum was limited.

Nevertheless, a number of notable new theatres were built during this era: Barcelona (1762); Frankfurt (1776); Mainz (1798); Montpellier (1804); London (1822); Erlangen (1826); Munich (1826); Dorpat (1827); Göttingen (1828); Tübingen (1832); Zurich (1842); Greifswald (1854); Berlin (1863); Fribourg (1867); Bonn (1872); Leipzig (1875); Prague (1876); Rostock (1876); Strasburg (1877); Breslau (1897); Marburg (1902); Basel (1921); Helsinki (1928); and Sofia (1929).

The evolution of audiovisual equipment gradually led to a revolution; anatomical auditoriums eventually became mere screening rooms. In 1872 the German physiologist Czermak (1828-1873) built what he called the 'Spectatorium' in Leipzig.

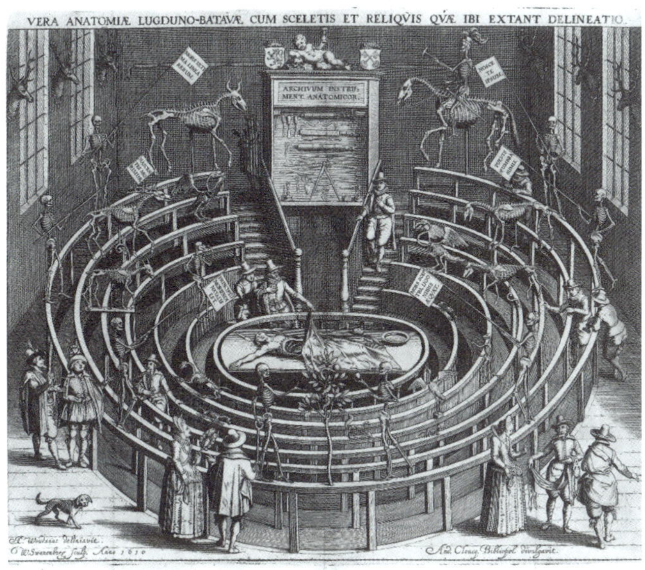

This institute, which comprised modern and comfortable audiovisual rooms, marked the definitive end of the traditional *Theatrum Anatomicum*.

05.

Berlin Institute for Medical Systems Biology (MDC-BIMSB)
Hannoversche Straße 28
U6 (Oranienburger Tor)

THE STAIRCASE OF THE MAX DELBRÜCK CENTER

A spectacular secret staircase

Built in 2019 by the architectural firm Staab Architekten, the Max Delbrück Center for Molecular Medicine (MDC) in Berlin, located a few minutes' walk from the Oranienburger Tor metro station and slightly set back from the street, does not immediately attract attention.

It nevertheless conceals an exceptional feature: the staircase of the Berlin Institute for Medical Systems Biology (BIMSB) building.

If you are able to obtain permission at reception, do not hesitate to explore this self-supporting helical staircase: On each floor, the perspective changes, offering a clearer understanding of its design.

On the ground floor, at the foot of the staircase, an installation composed of thousands of luminous spheres depicts the fall of particles over more than twenty metres. This striking display evokes the work of scientists on the infinitely small, making visible what usually escapes the human eye.

06.

Monbijouplatz
S3, 5, 7, 9 (Hackescher Markt)

THE STONE OF MONBIJOU PARK

The last stone

Two paths cross each other more or less in the middle of Monbijou Park. Nobody pays it much attention, but in the northeast angle is a large stone whose central oval medallion and symmetrical arabesques representing plants recall part of a Baroque façade. This stone is in fact the last remnant of the castle that stood here until 1951. This vestige clearly comes from the demolished façade of the castle, probably the ledge above the only row of windows, or the railing along the roof.

In the gardens of the Great Elector, where the very first potatoes of Brandenburg were planted (for their distinctive flowers), there used to be only a summer residence. In 1706 Frederick I had a small single-story castle built here for his mistress, the Duchess of Wartenberg. As of 1710, Crown Princess Dorothea, wife of Frederick William I of Prussia (the 'Soldier King'), occupied this small castle. Here, her son Fritz, the future Frederick the Great, could play the flute in peace without being bothered by his father.

Once Fritz became king, he designed for his mother a beautiful park around the castle, with its own jetty where sumptuous Rococo parties were held. She nicknamed her castle and park 'Mon Bijou' (from the French 'my jewel').

Under Emperor William II the pleasure palace slowly decayed and was converted into a museum dedicated to the Hohenzollern royal dynasty. Like West Germany, the German Democratic Republic was keen to make a clear break from its past, and in 1951 the government had the castle demolished.

07.

Sophienstraße 18
U8 (Weinmeisterstraße)

THE HANDSHAKE ON SOPHIENSTRAßE

Let's shake hands, comrade!

With its beautifully restored façade, the house at 18 Sophienstraße stands out from its rather gloomy neighbours. It is undoubtedly due to its communist past that this house drew particular attention in the days of the German Democratic Republic: behind the arcades of the entrance porch in its inner courtyard is where, during the revolution of November 1918, the first Spartacist protests took place after Karl Liebknecht and Rosa Luxemburg made their powerful speeches. The emblem that embodies this moment, seen here on the wall above the pillar between the porch's two larges arcades, is a handshake.

The interlocked hands on the façade are only indirectly linked to those of the Socialist Unity Party of Germany (SED), formed in 1946 when the SPD (Social Democratic Party) and the KPD (Communist Party) merged. Indeed, the handshake emblem existed well before that and was linked to the Berlin Artisans' Association.

Founded in 1846, the Berlin Artisans' Association aimed to give the working classes a voice. Members voted for their own committee and together they set the association's objectives.

Two years after its creation, the association already had 1,000 members. Its initial aim was the intellectual education of artisans, to enable them to think and act independently while flattering the incumbent authority so as to avoid state censorship: the association's bylaws stated that moral and intellectual life within the handicrafts sector should foster patriotism, encourage respect and compliance with the laws, as well as love for and faithfulness to the monarch. In reality, the association's original emblem represented two hands holding a sword.

With 3,000 members, the Berlin Artisans' Association was in fact a breeding ground for future revolutionaries, and it turned into a secret army of the working class, proving particularly active during the 1848 revolution. In light of the difficulties establishing a democracy during the Frankfurt Parliament, the first elected National Assembly came together in Saint Paul's Church. It quickly quenched the popular uprising that could not resist the retaliation of the King's well-armed troops. Political associations were forbidden in 1849, and it was only in 1859 that the association was allowed to reunite. On this occasion, the sword, considered too martial, was removed from the emblem above the arcades of the entrance.

Despite this, the association remained very political. In fact, as history has shown, it remained so political that the Nazis also decided to dissolve it.

HANDWERKE

08.

Memhardstraße 8
U2, 5, 8 (Alexanderplatz)

HONI'S WINDOW

Why does this building façade only have one window?

Based on the number of bells at the entrance, the block at number 2 Memhardstraße in Mitte includes 120 apartments. The 'Memi' building – as it is affectionately known among its inhabitants – stands 30 metres tall and 40 metres wide. There is a legend linked to one of its windows.

Despite the hundreds of windows dotting its façades, the lone window on the eighth floor, on the side overlooking Alexander Platz, clearly stands out. If neighbours are to be believed, this window looks out of the apartment of one of the daughters of the Chairman of the State Council, Erich Honecker, who many nicknamed Honi. But did the apartment belong to his daughter Erika, born from his first marriage, or his daughter Sonja, born of an illegitimate union? Whatever the answer, the person occupying this apartment was evidently able to add a window to her initially windowless bathroom. Some even say that Erich Honecker himself monitored his people's activities from this observation post.

According to another source, the apartment in question belonged to the daughter of Erich Mielke, head of the East German Ministry for State Security, the Stasi. When asked about it, the head of the Berlin-Mitte housing association responded that the housing plans are allegedly different from one floor to another, especially among the top floors. According to him, the window has always been there. But oddly enough, he was referring to an apartment on the ninth floor, whereas the window in question is located on the eighth.

Not so long ago, drug dealers would ply their trade around the four entrances of the building and in its stairwells, which were also sought-after places to do drugs discreetly. It has been said that the problem was resolved by changing the lighting in the corridors and stairwells, making it more difficult for drug users to see their veins and inject themselves.

1. Berliner
Motorrad - Museum

SOUTH MITTE

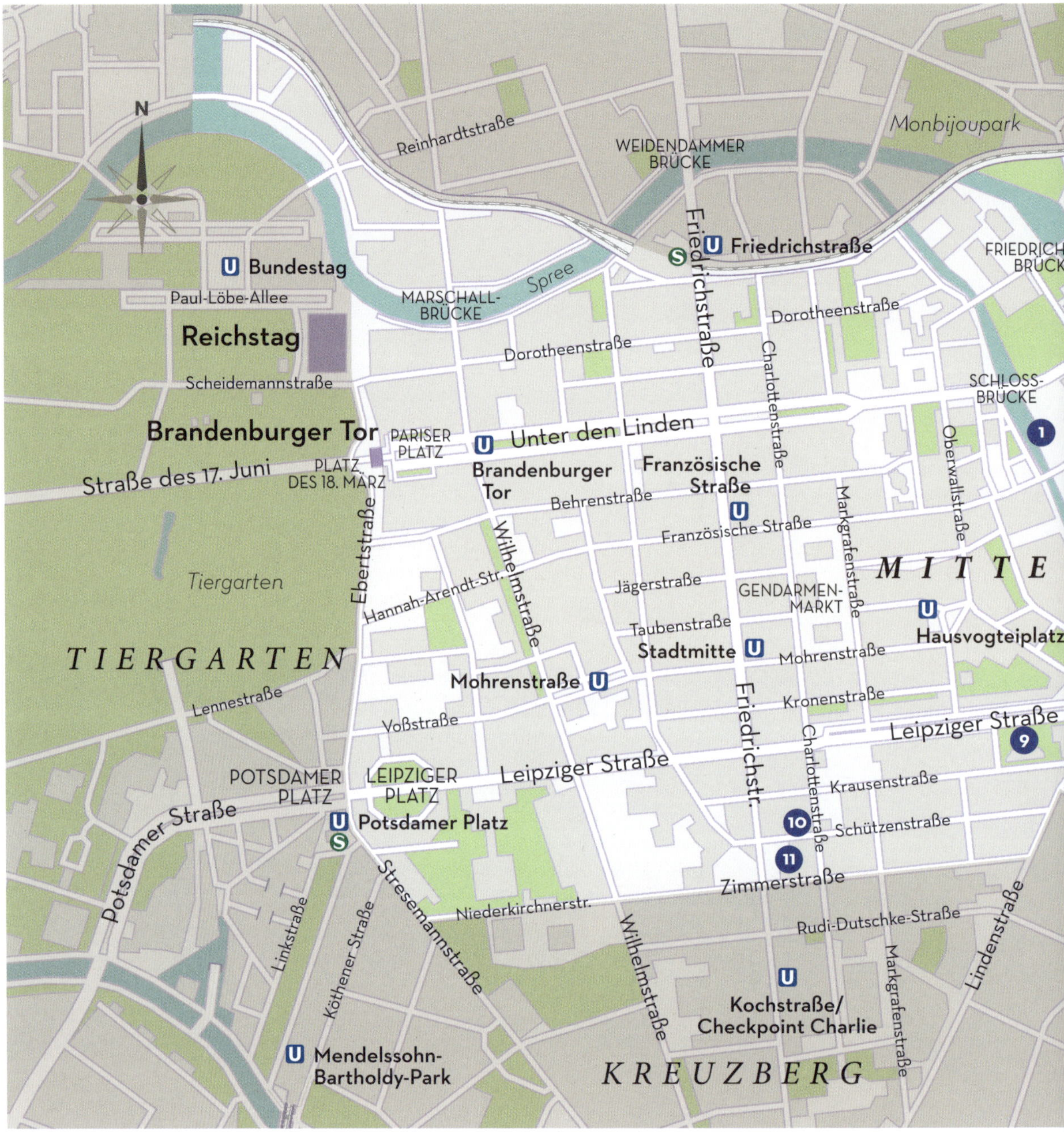
N
Reinhardtstraße
WEIDENDAMMER BRÜCKE
Monbijoupark
Bundestag
Paul-Löbe-Allee
Reichstag
Scheidemannstraße
Spree
MARSCHALL-BRÜCKE
Friedrichstraße
Friedrichstraße
FRIEDRICH BRÜCK
Dorotheenstraße
Dorotheenstraße
Charlottenstraße
SCHLOSS-BRÜCKE
1
Brandenburger Tor
PARISER PLATZ
Unter den Linden
Straße des 17. Juni
PLATZ DES 18. MÄRZ
Brandenburger Tor
Französische Straße
Behrenstraße
Oberwallstraße
Ebertstraße
Französische Straße
Markgrafenstraße
Wilhelmstraße
MITTE
Tiergarten
Hannah-Arendt-Str.
Jägerstraße
GENDARMEN-MARKT
Hausvogteiplatz
Taubenstraße
Stadtmitte
Mohrenstraße
TIERGARTEN
Mohrenstraße
Kronenstraße
Lennestraße
Leipziger Straße
Voßstraße
Friedrichstr.
Charlottenstraße
9
POTSDAMER PLATZ
LEIPZIGER PLATZ
Leipziger Straße
Krausenstraße
Potsdamer Straße
Potsdamer Platz
10
Schützenstraße
11
Zimmerstraße
Stresemannstraße
Niederkirchnerstr.
Rudi-Dutschke-Straße
Lindenstraße
Linkstraße
Köthener Straße
Wilhelmstraße
Markgrafenstraße
Kochstraße/ Checkpoint Charlie
Mendelssohn-Bartholdy-Park
KREUZBERG

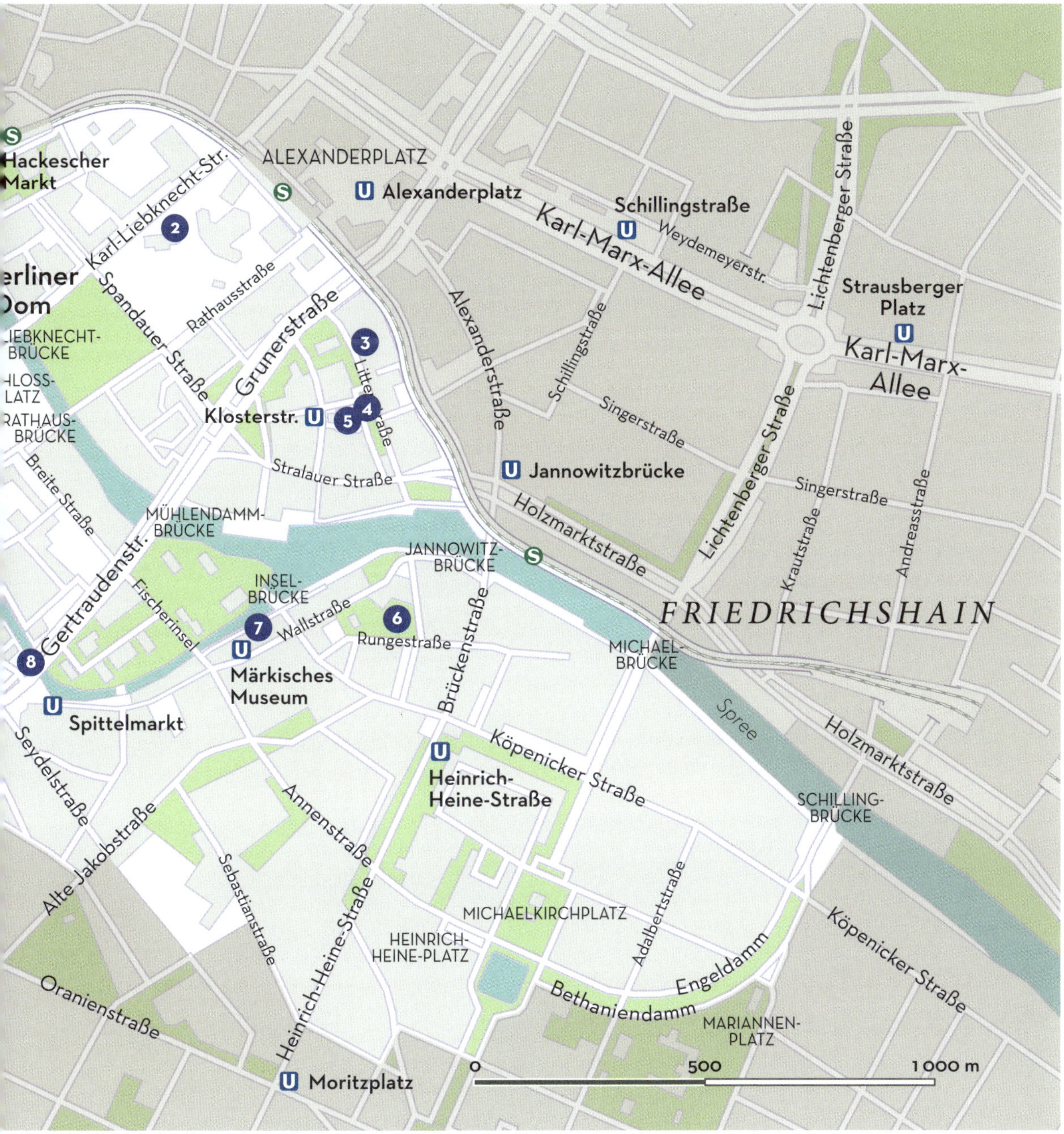

07. ERMELER HOUSE BAS-RELIEF *p. 48*

08. GERTRUDE'S MOUSE *p. 50*

09. HISTORICAL MILESTONE ON DÖNHOFF PLATZ *p. 52*

10. THE MICHAELSEN PALACE *p. 56*

11. ALFANDARY HOUSE BAS-RELIEFS *p. 58*

01.

Lustgarten, Unter den Linden 1
S3, 5, 7, 9 (Hackescher Markt) / U2 (Hausvogteiplatz)

DOLPHIN SCULPTURE

The last remnant of a historic balustrade

Near the Schlossbrücke (palace bridge), on the south-west side of Lustgarten park, there stands a rather lonesome-looking sculpture of a dolphin in a rusty cast-iron frame. The Lustgarten dolphin is indeed the last of the dolphin sculptures that used to decorate the balustrades of the palace bridge after it underwent refurbishment works under the supervision of the architect Karl Friedrich Schinkel in 1824. The bridge's current dolphins are actually just copies.
Schinkel's enhancement works of 1824 were, for the most part, a response to the 1823 catastrophe that took place here (see below).

AN UNLIKELY DROWNING

On 16 November 1823, the Prussian crown prince Frederick William and his wife Elisabeth of Bavaria were to be married in the palace's chapel in Berlin. To celebrate their arrival at the Berlin palace, Frederick William III requested that a large parade and a party in the Lustgarten be organised. The palace's new bridge, whose balustrade had not yet been fitted, was to be inaugurated at the same time with the crossing of the royal couple in a golden carriage. Nobody thought about the audience.
Nothing more than a wooden walkway nailed to the bridge was installed to welcome the onlookers. On the other hand, the area reserved for the couple was large enough to fit seven carriages! Quarrels started to erupt for the best spot on the walkway, and the inevitable happened: the makeshift balustrade broke and the spectators fell into the canal. On top of the fact that many of them did not know how to swim, their heavy winter clothing hampered their movements. As a result, some 22 onlookers drowned that day.
However, the unfortunate incident did not seem to weigh on the conscience of King Frederick William III who had none the less organised a meal for the poor as a gesture to celebrate the wedding. Indeed, on his instructions, the publication of obituaries in the local newspapers was forbidden so as not to upset the newlyweds. It is only after the families complained to the ministry in charge that the death notices were eventually authorised.

© Dieter Burgmann

02.

Karl-Liebknecht-Straße 8
S3, 5, 7, 9 (Alexanderplatz)

THE WHITE CROSS OF SAINT MARY'S CHURCH

God does not forget

Dating back to 1270, the medieval Church of Saint Mary is hardly a secret. But not many are aware of the discrete cross carved in white stone to the left of the main entrance.

Long ago, the rival houses of Wittelsbach and Habsburg were competing for control in the Holy Roman Empire. Pope John XXII, an enemy of the Wittelsbachs, stirred up discord across the towns within their territories.

It was in this context that on 16 August 1324 (or 1325) the Provost Nikolaus von Bernau made a passionate speech in Saint Mary's Church against the young Prince Elector of the Wittelsbach family, a speech that was to prove fatal to him.

Admittedly, there is no certainty that the provost was even able to hold his sermon in the church. Was he dragged out of the building to be put to death? Did patricians close to the Wittelsbach family plan the coup and incite the people to perpetrate this abomination? Or was the assassination ordered by the margrave himself? Nobody knows for sure, but one thing is certain: Nikolaus was beaten to death by the mob and his body was burned on site. It is even said that the fire was lit a second time to get rid of the remains entirely.

The pope was furious, but it took a year for the sentence of excommunication he had promulgated in Avignon to reach Berlin. The divine services, access to the churches, the last sacraments, and the presence of a priest at weddings and funerals were now all forbidden by His Holiness. However, the Franciscans and Dominicans of Cölln were still able to perform their pastoral responsibilities to the community that had not been involved either in these quarrels or in the assassination perpetrated by a few fanatics. This time, the civil jurisdiction, which should have dealt with the case of lynching by convening a judicial assembly in the old town hall to make a court ruling, kept its silence. As a sign of repentance, a white cross and an ever-burning lamp were installed in the church.

The purchase of papal indulgences brought absolution to the city and cleared it from the smear that had plagued it up until 1345. The lamp that was supposed to burn eternally has since disappeared, leaving five small holes in the white cross.

03.

Littenstraße 12–17
U2 (Klosterstraße)

FOYER OF THE BERLIN COURTHOUSE

Incredible architecture inside and out

Whilst the Berlin Regional Court (Landgericht Berlin) building itself is not exactly a secret in Berlin, most people who are familiar with it have no idea that it is open to visitors. Yet it houses one of the most beautiful interiors in the whole city.

After passing through security at the entrance on Littenstraße (a passport or ID card is sufficient), visitors are greeted by a spectacular sight: a circular hall 30.50 metres high, adorned with rich decorations blending several styles.

Particularly noteworthy are the sandstone columns and two magnificent staircases adorned with knights in armour, as well as the white wrought-iron balustrades of the staircases, typical of Jugendstil (Art Nouveau).

As you ascend to the upper floors, you can admire the superb chandelier suspended in the centre of the hall, as well as the atrium in its entirety (1,000 m^2).

Opened in 1904, the building was designed by architects Paul Thoemer, Rudolf Mönnich and Otto Schmalz to house the civil division of the Berlin Regional Court and the Mitte District Court. With its five kilometres of corridors and 3,000 windows, it was one of the city's largest buildings.

The building suffered extensive damage during the Second World War and was partially rebuilt after the war, although in 1968–69 an entire wing that had not been damaged was demolished to make way for Grunerstraße.

Having also housed the GDR Supreme Court, it currently accommodates several civil chambers of the Regional Court as well as the Court of Appeal of the Berlin Regional Court.

© Ansgar Koreng

04.

Waisenstraße 14–16
S3, 5, 7, 9 (Alexanderplatz) / U2 (Klosterstraße)

REMAINS OF THE CITY WALLS

The last traces of the old city wall

The limits of the old town of Cölln run south from Alexanderplatz, and, if on foot, traces can be seen of the oldest constructions in today's Berlin.

Go past the 13th century Notre-Dame church before walking left around Rotes Rathaus, then go down the Jüdenstraße and across the Grünstraße. The centre of the former Jewish quarter, the Große Jüdenhof, is now a car park in the town centre.

If you walk down the Grünstraße to the left, you will come to the church of the Franciscan monastery, in ruins since the last war – traffic drives over its foundations today.

Turn right into a quiet street called Littenstraße to discover the oldest traces of Berlin's architecture that are still standing: the remains of the medieval city wall built around 1250 and which measured 2.5 kilometres in those days, surrounding the 70 hectares of Cölln and Berlin.

On the small section where the streets of Littenstraße and Waisenstraße run parallel to each other, these remains were uncovered when the ruins of the bombed houses covering them were cleared away in 1948. The Zur letzten Instanz inn building was also part of the old city walls and was used as a Wiekhaus, a type of lookout post which was sometimes built into the wall. In 1621, one of the Prince Elector's grooms set up an inn there, the earliest ancestor of the current café-restaurant.

We can get a closer look at what remains of the first walls in the front, back and inside the café: 3 to 6 feet thick (around 1 to 2 metres), they have vertical parts which were added over time and were built either on relatively rough stones or slotted tightly together. The bricks were used to raise the part of the original wall (around two metres high), which is made up of stone rubble taken from fields, giving it a total height of four or five metres. Some crenelations were added here and there. In addition to the many Wiekhäuser, towers measuring up to 25 metres high were built randomly along it, providing a lookout to spot approaching enemies.

In front of the new wall (near today's Littenstraße), two 15-metre wide ditches, separated by ramparts of 7.5 to 10 metres wide, were dug to slow down enemy advances. As with all urban defence systems, there were *trous-de-loup* (in German, literally 'bear traps' – for the future heraldic animal). Some years ago, it was still possible to see traces of the prints of small carnivores, which had been cooked into the red bricks of the monastery. Today, they are being slowly worn away.

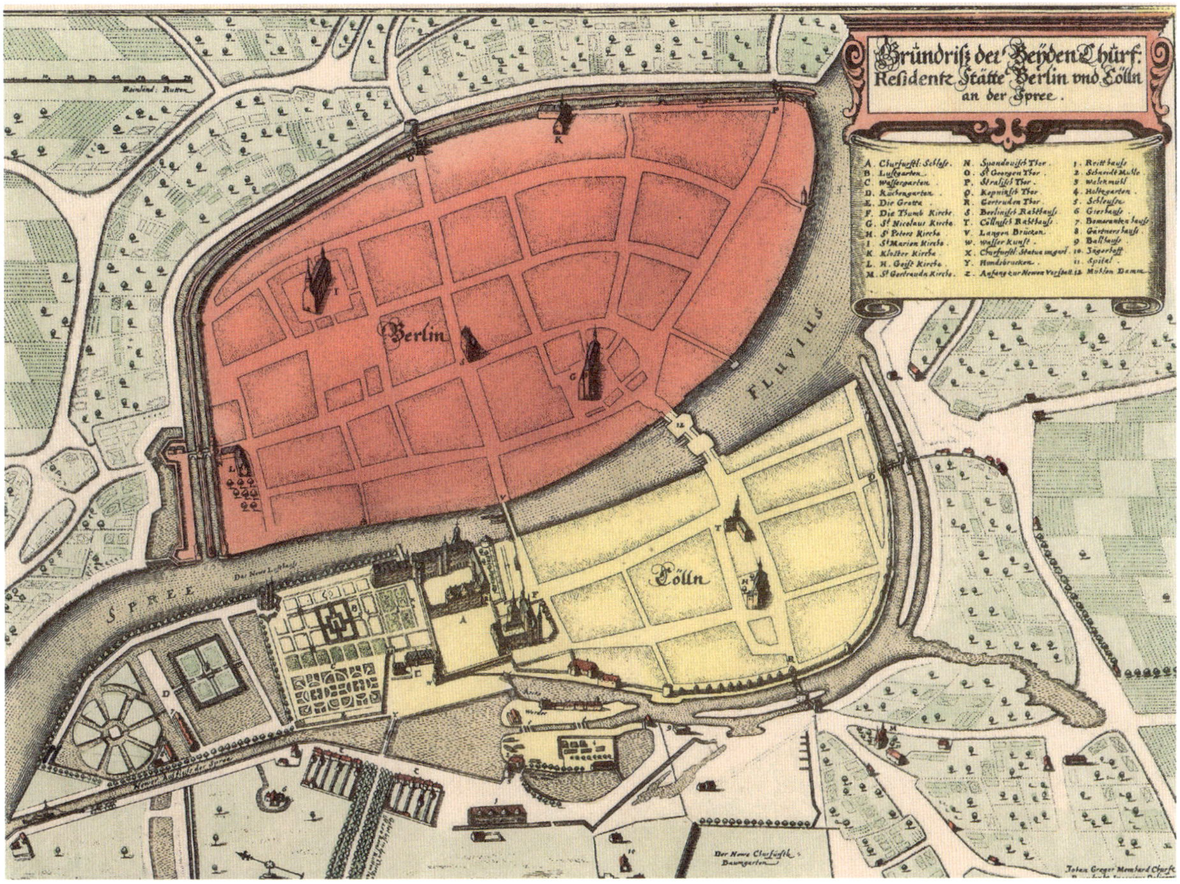
Grundriß der Beyden Churf: Residentz Stätte Berlin und Cölln an der Spree.
A. Churfurstl: Schloss.
B. Lustgarten.
C. Wassergarten.
D. Küchengarten.
E. Die Grotta.
F. Die Thumb Kirche.
G. St Nicolaus Kirche.
H. St Peters Kirche.
I. St Marien Kirche.
K. Kloster Kirche.
L. H. Geist Kirche.
M. St Gertraudn Kirche.
N. Spandauisch Thor.
O. St Georgen Thor.
P. Stralisch Thor.
Q. Kopnisch Thor.
R. Gertruden Thor.
S. Berlinisch Rahthaus.
T. Cöllnisch Rahthaus.
V. Langen Brücken.
W. Wasser Kunst.
X. Churfurstl: Statua ungert.
Y. Hundsbrucken.
Z. Anfang zur Newen Vorstatt.
1. Reitthaus.
2. Schneidt Mülle.
3. Walckmüll.
4. Holtzgarten.
5. Schleuse.
6. Gierhaus.
7. Bomaranken haus.
8. Gärtners haus.
9. Ballhaus.
10. Jägerhoff.
11. Spital.
12. Mühlen Damm.
Berlin
Cölln
Spree
Fluvius

05.

Klosterstraße 66
U2 (Klosterstraße)

THE CRYPT OF THE PAROCHIALKIRCHE

A perspective of eternity

The crypt can be reached by a narrow, stone spiral staircase a few yards away from the vast nave of the Baroque parish church (Parochialkirche) on Klosterstraße, which was built between 1695 and 1703.
The only crypt in Berlin containing the tombs of lesser nobility and wealthy bourgoisie, its cross-shaped aisles follow the same pattern used in Baroque religious buildings. Stemming from the axes of the cross, some thirty tombs are arranged down the sides. Each burial vault is closed by a simple wooden, slatted gate, giving a glimpse of the interior and allowing some ventilation.
The good ventilation system, which made the Parochialkirche crypt special from the very beginning, has, in fact, largely mummified the fully dressed remains of those who had paid for their resting place there. The mummies were discovered during the restoration of this crypt, which is the only one of its kind in Europe. On the guided tours, visitors can get a closer look at the burial vaults with their stone tombs and wooden coffins and some photos explaining the mummies in more detail.
Visitors can also see the very modern dress, made in a golden-coloured silk satin fabric, with its plunging neckline that was worn by Baroness Louise Albertine von Grappendorf (who died around 1750 at the age of 24). As her funeral took place in winter, her fragile skin was not perforated by maggots.
There is also the cat (also mummified) – lying in the arms of Lorenz Christoph Schneider, the commissioner of the Mint who died in 1715, or the area filled with children's coffins and a vault with a coffin with a window, which had been added to overcome the fear of being buried alive.
During this tour, the macabre story of Else the Red is also referred to. If ever the annual payment (the equivalent of about 40,000 Euros today) was not paid, the bones were buried during the night in the little parish cemetery, where commoners are covered with earth and where robes, as precious as they may have been, turn into humus.
During the 20th century, the crypt, which was not protected, was desecrated countless times. Grave robbers in search of jewellery cut through the gloves of the mummies and the students at the Charité Hospital, encouraged by their professors, used it as a free supply of human skulls. The crypt was finally walled up, which prevented the air from circulating and caused mould to form that archaeologists sometimes refer to as 'the pharaoh's curse'.

06.

Am Köllnischen Park 5
U2 (Märkisches Museum)

THE WUSTERHAUSISCHER BÄR

The last witness of Berlin's fortifications

A curious little tower of bricks stands proudly in Köllnischer Park. The sculpture, which is capped with a roof in the shape of a salad bowl, is no more than 5 metres high from top to bottom. Its modest interior is closed off with a gate and cut open with an arrow slit. The inscription 'Wusterhausischer Bär 1718', which was put there in the days of the Prussian king, Frederick William I ('soldier king' and father of 'Old Fritz'), does not seem to mean very much. Like most of the sculptures and other architectural remains from old Berlin which are gathered in this park, it no longer stands on its original spot. This place is used as a refuge for stone artefacts which have had to make way for others, without being given a new space in the buildings of the Märkisches Museum (the museum of Mark Brandenburg) or in its interior courtyard.

In the year 2000, visitors could still see an authentic brown bear, the heraldic animal of Berlin, in the bear pit in this park at mealtimes. But the *Bär* (which means 'bear' in German and is pronounced 'Behr') of the sculpture has absolutely nothing to do with bears. It would seem that the etymology of the word Bär comes from the medieval Latin *barra* or 'barrier'. They are constructions that were part of the defensive arsenal that was also called *Wehr* in German. A Bär was a specific dam of fortifications around Berlin. The dams were set up in the moats, the walls of which were equipped with a defensive tower which were used to protect these moats and block any attacks or sieges that were waged on the fortifications. The tower covered the entire length of the dam, from one side to the other, so effectively that whoever tried to get round it would invariably fall into the water. Of the three pseudo bears (*Bären*, in fact *Wehren* and therefore dams) which were operating in Berlin's defensive moats, it was the Bär of Wusterhausen which best stood the test of time. The fortifications were taken down in the 18th century, but the dam continued to operate in the moat known as the green moat (Grüner Graben) by regulating the water coming into the mill. As the dam was on the road to the small town of Königs Wusterhausen, it was called the Wusterhausischer Bär. When the green moat and the dam were filled in, in 1883 and 1884, the tower known as the Wusterhausischer Bär was the only thing left standing in the new Jakobsstraße street. In the plan of conservation measures recommended by the Märkisches Museum, it was dismantled and rebuilt in Köllnischer Park. This was added to the inscription of 1718: 'built in the middle of the first green moat behind bastion VI'.

The Bär/Wehr/bear is today the last trace of the, once immense, fortifications of Berlin, which were so impenetrable that they never suffered attacks or sieges.

07.

Märkisches Ufer 10
U2 (Märkisches Museum)

ERMELER HOUSE BAS-RELIEF

Slaves to enrich Berlin

Located on the Friedrichs-Gracht quay, the Ermeler House was named after an old tradition typical of port cities. The beautiful bas-relief above the main entrance door depicts a tropical landscape and half-naked men and women harvesting tobacco by hand.

Berlin merchants made a fortune from the tobacco trade. Wilhelm Ferdinand Ermeler, who bought this house in 1824 from a tobacco trader named Neumann, wrote in his diary: 'I started with 100 thaler and now, at the age of 56, I already have more than 200,000 [...] Fully deserved.'

Along the bas-relief, which already existed at the time Ermeler bought the house, images show tobacco being imported by ships, themselves guarded by white Europeans.

To the right, the two churches of the Gendarmenmarkt indicate that the leaves were destined for sale in Berlin.

In the 1690s alone, slave traders in Berlin (the place of residence of prince-electors and where slave trading had been authorised since the days of the Grand Elector in the 17th century) deported more than 20,000 men, women and children from Africa and sent them to plantations in the southern colonies of the United States.

For a while, Prussia even outnumbered its Dutch and French competitors in terms of human trafficking. At the time, Berlin's rich merchants viewed Africans as savages, animals that could be captured and exploited without remorse. This is in fact what Pastor Gossner used to do through his missions with the (Moravian) Bohemian Bethlehem Church in Berlin.

This work of art, along with the street name that caused controversy in the 1990s (Mohrenstraße), is now considered by many to be racist.

Built during the 18th century at number 11 Breiten Straße, the Ermeler House was destroyed in 1966-1967 and rebuilt in its current location in 1968-1969. During its reconstruction, the original bas-relief was replaced.

08.

Gertraudenbrücke
U2 (Spittelmarkt)

GERTRUDE'S MOUSE

For a full wallet ...

Just a stone's throw from its original spot, the beautiful statue of Saint Gertrude was reinstalled in 2021 at the heart of the Gertraudenbrücke, on the canal's western bank.

The statue shows a nun offering a comforting drink to a gaunt pilgrim, easily identified by his staff. The contrast between the nun's dignified posture and the pilgrim's crouched, submissive stance makes it clear she is no ordinary woman.

This is Saint Gertrude (c. 625–659), who oversaw the education of young women at the monastery of Nivelles, a major pilgrimage site founded by her mother, Itta.

Tirelessly devoted to caring for the poor, the sick, widows, travellers, pilgrims, and prisoners, Gertrude became the patron saint of many medieval hospices.

In the Middle Ages, a hospice was not only a place for the poor or elderly, but also a religious guesthouse for pilgrims and wayfarers. One such hospice was established in the 15th century outside the old Teltow Gate in Cölln, on what was then the Teltow Bridge. It was named the *Gertrud Krankenhaus* (Gertrude Hospice).

In 1896, sculptor Rudolf Siemering completed the statue commissioned by the city council to commemorate this hospice. The wooden bridge crossing the Spree Canal, as well as the former city gate, were both renamed in her honour – although no one really knows why 'Gertrud' became 'Gertraude' in the process. When Berlin and Cölln merged, the gate vanished, and in 1853, the hospice became a hospital before relocating to Kreuzberg.

Legend has it that Gertrude chased away the mice that infested her hospice. In fact, a rodent-repelling mixture once known as *Gertrudenwasser* (Gertrude's Water) was named after her.

A old saying went, *If you want to eat fat beans, don't forget Gertrude!* To ensure a good harvest, farmers would make an offering at her chapel. Thanks to her triumph over rats and mice, Saint Gertrude also became associated with protection against disease and epidemics such as the plague, as well as the patron saint of gardeners.

And in Berlin today, the legend lives on: touching the mouse sculpted at the saint's feet is said to bring financial fortune.

© Tom Wolf

09.

Leipziger Straße 49
U2 (Spittelmarkt)

HISTORICAL MILESTONE ON DÖNHOFF PLATZ

Berlin's level zero

At number 49 Leipziger Straße, in front of the Spittelkolonnade of Dönhoff square, stands a good-sized obelisk which is often overlooked, however, as passers-by think it is part of the Spittelkolonnade.

This obelisk, dating from 1979, is in fact a copy of a level 'zero' milestone (*Null-Meilenstein*) which indicated the point from which the Prussian postal service calculated its distances from Berlin. The original milestone was installed in 1730 a few metres away from where it stands today. At the end of the Thirty Years' War (1618-1648), desolation reigned in Brandenburg. Berlin's population was decimated, falling from 13,000 to a mere 4,000 inhabitants. Brandenburg's economy was in serious decline. To save it, Elector Frederick William of Brandenburg (1620-1688) drew up postal routes lining the main trade routes of the region. Some of these axes can still be seen today and have even become the famous federal roads in the German capital (notably numbers one and five, inaugurated respectively in 1646 and 1660).

The region's first milestones, used for precise calculations depending on the distance to be driven, delivery deadlines and postage costs, also date back to this time. They also indicated the postal charges, as the post was delivered by the famous stagecoaches (*Postkutsche*) used by travellers. From 1800, these roads became paved streets known as *Chaussees* (the name given to Chaussee Straße in Mitte, one of the capital's first two paved streets, with Bundesstraße 1 leading to Potsdam, a section of which still bears the name Potsdamer Chaussee). All the users of these fast roads, except for the sovereign and the postal service, were charged a tax based on the military milestones.

Distances were calculated from so-called 'zero' points, indicated by granite obelisks that were placed at different entrances to the city, which, surrounded by moats and bastions, then stretched for only a few square kilometres. Although it is difficult to be absolutely sure, it would seem that there were in fact at least two 'zero' points: one in the north of the city, in front of the Oranienburg gate, and one in the south.

The obelisk on Dönhoff Platz originally stood on the south-west side of the city, in front of the Leipzig gate (which gives its name to today's Leipziger Straße, onto which this gate opened out).

Starting from these obelisks, the milestones were placed at intervals of one mile and half a mile (and, according to some records, a quarter of a mile). The Prussian mile measured 24,000 footsteps (around 7.5 km), in other words, the average distance originally travelled by a stagecoach in two hours.

For more information about where to find the military milestones in Berlin, see the following double page.

BERLIN'S OTHER MILITARY MILESTONES

In addition to the copy of the Null-Meilenstein on Dönhoff Platz, twelve military milestones still stand discreetly in the streets of the German capital:

1. At 63 Hauptstraße, Schöneberg
2. At 44 Potsdamer Straße, Zehlendorf
3. At 42 Königstraße, Wannsee
4. At 7 Spandauer Damm, Charlottenburg
5. In front of 220 Spandauer Damm, Ruhwald
6. On the Lichtenberg bridge (Lichtenberger Brücke), Lichtenberg
7. On Alt-Mahlsdorf street (in front of 109, on the other side of the street), Mahlsdorf
8. On the corner of Gabrielenstraße and An der Mühle, Alt-Tegel
9. On Ruppiner Chaussee (in front of 377a, on the other side of the street), Hennigdorf
10. On the corner of Falkenberger Chaussee and Pablo-Picasso-Straße, Neu-Hohenschönhausen
11. At 169 Waltersdorfer Chaussee, Rudow
12. Opposite 66 Buschkrugallee, Britz

IIII
MEILEN
von
BERLIN

10.

Schützenstraße 6–6A
U6 (Kochstraße Checkpoint Charlie)

THE MICHAELSEN PALACE

A magnificent example of German Art Nouveau

At No. 6 Schützenstraße, the Michaelsen-Palais, also known as the Hotel Roter Adler, is one of the most representative examples of German Art Nouveau (Jugendstil) in central Berlin. It is easy to overlook, however, as the most interesting part of its façade is located at the very top of the building.

Among the many figures depicted there, just below a massive representation of the Greek god Hermes, are two famous men: Charlemagne (on the left) and Emperor William I (on the right). Between them, Saint George struggles to slay the dragon (a symbol of good fighting against evil), while the bust of the 'Iron Chancellor ' Otto von Bismarck stands out clearly, lower down on the right, at the level of the pediment.

The building was constructed between 1903 and 1907 by the Berlin architect Otto Michaelsen, after whom it was named, at the request of the contractor Emil Voigt. Barely a year after construction was completed, Voigt had to sell the building due to financial difficulties. The building was subsequently acquired by the Swiss insurance company Winterthur, which set up its offices there. During World War II, the Michaelsen-Palais was used, among other things, as the criminal court of the Chamber of Commerce, as well as a hotel. It was after the fall of the Berlin Wall that Winterthur regained possession of the building, which was renovated in the early 2000s.

Note the entrance gate at No. 6, one of the most beautiful in the city.

© Sliwecki, Marek

11.

Zimmerstraße 79–80
U6 (Kochstraße/Checkpoint Charlie)

ALFANDARY HOUSE BAS-RELIEFS

Mythology on ceramics

Just a few metres away from Checkpoint Charlie, and swamped with hordes of tourists, stands a house built of partially vitrified bricks known as 'Dutch' or 'clinker', the main attraction of which is a narrow frieze on the front. Before reunification, this house was the editorial office of East Berlin's newspaper Neue Zeit.

After the Second World War, it was also home to the Union Verlag publishing house's readers' office. The writer Johannes Bobrowski worked there for a while. One wall of the house was part of the border between East and West Berlin and faced part of a demarcation zone.

Today, the advertising sign for the Neue Zeit no longer shines on the front. The house has been painstakingly restored to its 1914 original condition, except the last floor that was added under the rafters with windows overlooking Zimmerstraße.

In those days, this building which was built for the Sephardic Alfandary family, who ran an import-export business, caused a real sensation. In Berlin's directory, the Alfandarys (Jacques manager for Istanbul, Moïse dealing with London, Salomon and Raphaël with Berlin) advertised 'Persian rugs, wholesale embroidery and products imported from the East.'

The German architect, John Martens, who was the project manager for the work, specialised in construction ceramics and had developed a new manufacturing process which made it particularly weather resistant. He used it to make the decorative frieze on the front of the house. Its main role was to detract attention from

a certain aesthetic imbalance: to the right, four doors were added to the two floors, opening out onto the warehouses. Two barely perceptible women were also added to the central mullion of two of the windows on the second floor.

Hans Schmidt, who designed this frieze, placed characters and symbols side by side like hieroglyphics. The characters – three women and a man – are depicted lying down as there was not enough space to show them standing.

They are interspersed with symbols of perseverance and economic activity (a hive) and abundance (a basket of fruit). A child brings flowers, and a small pet dog lies near a sunflower; the second (Leda?) raises her hand against a swan; the third seems to be facing a goat (maybe a satyr). The divinities are represented by a large head, containing another small one in its mouth. The sleeping man at the far right hand end seems to be dreaming of a golden age: a gnome holding a coconut tree palm in his hand and pulling a minecart full of ore.

KREUZBERG

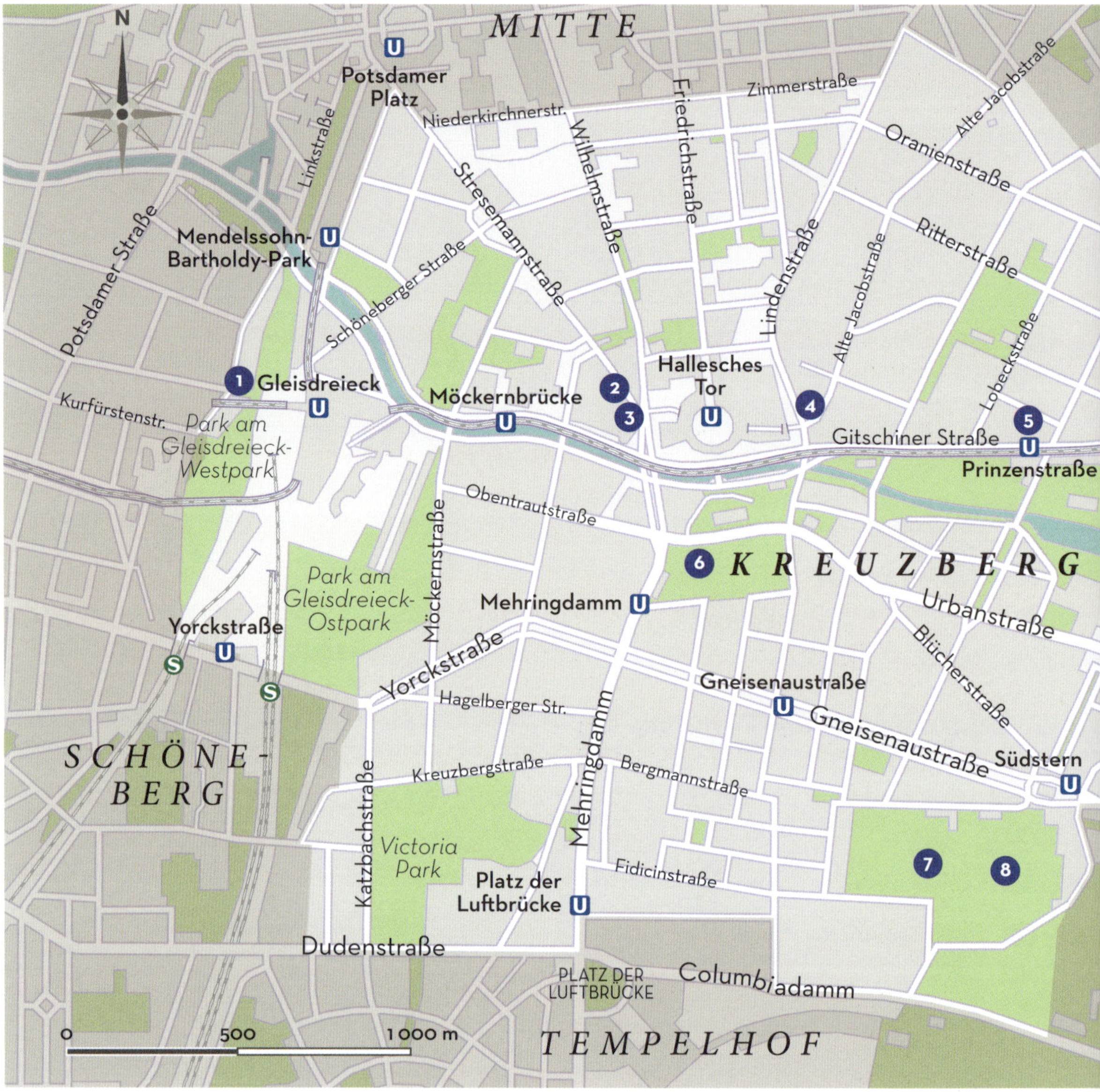
N
MITTE
Potsdamer Platz
Niederkirchnerstr.
Zimmerstraße
Friedrichstraße
Wilhelmstraße
Stresemannstraße
Linkstraße
Alte Jacobstraße
Oranienstraße
Ritterstraße
Potsdamer Straße
Mendelssohn-Bartholdy-Park
Schöneberger Straße
Lindenstraße
Alte Jacobstraße
Lobeckstraße
Hallesches Tor
Gleisdreieck
Möckernbrücke
Kurfürstenstr.
Park am Gleisdreieck-Westpark
Gitschiner Straße
Prinzenstraße
Obentrautstraße
Möckernstraße
KREUZBERG
Park am Gleisdreieck-Ostpark
Mehringdamm
Urbanstraße
Yorckstraße
Blücherstraße
Yorckstraße
Hagelberger Str.
Gneisenaustraße
Gneisenaustraße
Südstern
SCHÖNE-BERG
Kreuzbergstraße
Bergmannstraße
Mehringdamm
Katzbachstraße
Victoria Park
Platz der Luftbrücke
Fidicinstraße
Dudenstraße
PLATZ DER LUFTBRÜCKE
Columbiadamm
0
500
1 000 m
TEMPELHOF

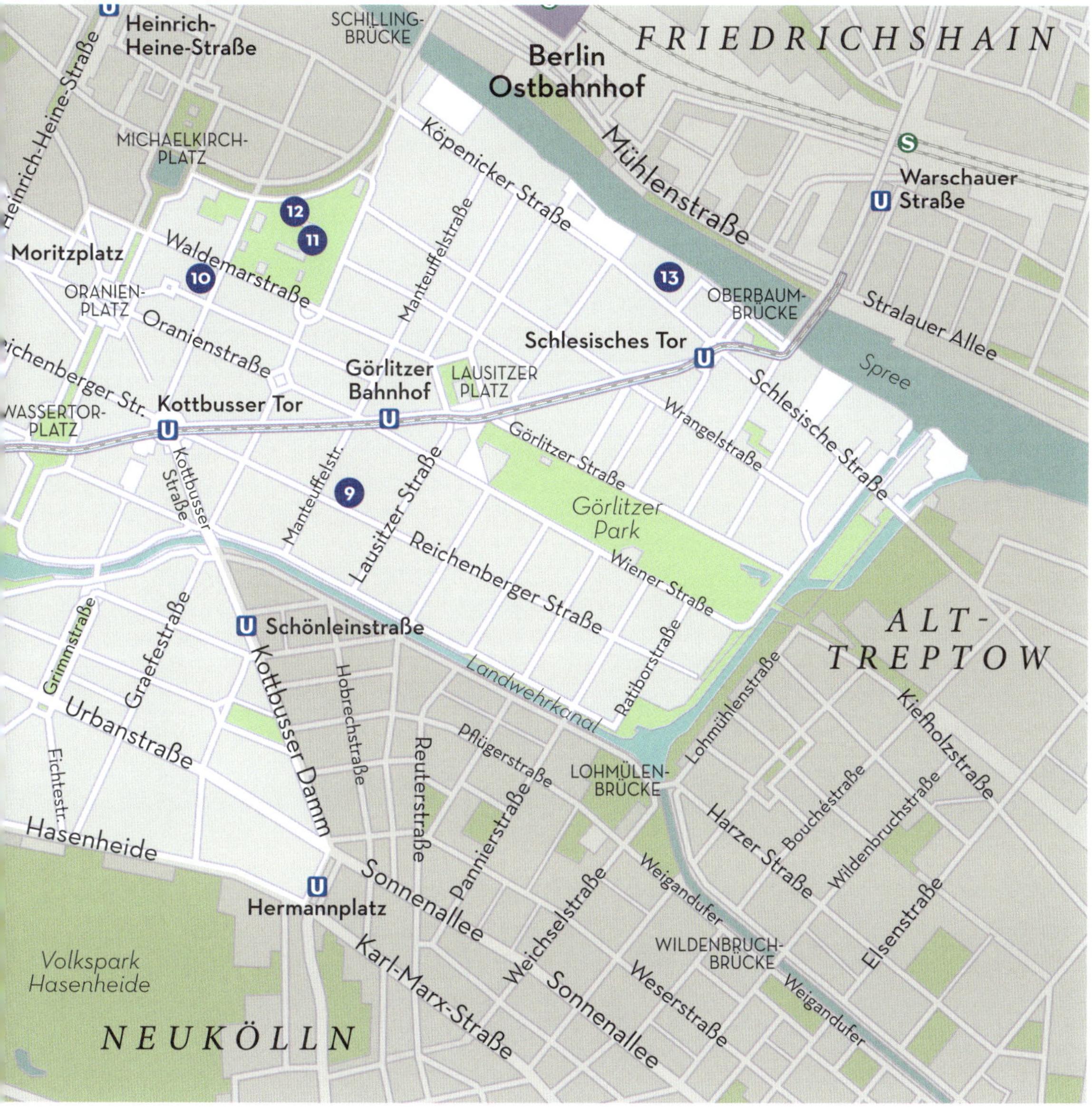
FRIEDRICHSHAIN
Heinrich-Heine-Straße
SCHILLING-BRÜCKE
Berlin Ostbahnhof
Heinrich-Heine-Straße
MICHAELKIRCH-PLATZ
Köpenicker Straße
Mühlenstraße
Warschauer Straße
Moritzplatz
Waldemarstraße
Manteuffelstraße
ORANIEN-PLATZ
Oranienstraße
OBERBAUM-BRÜCKE
Stralauer Allee
Schlesisches Tor
Spree
Görlitzer Bahnhof
LAUSITZER PLATZ
Kottbusser Tor
WASSERTOR-PLATZ
Wrangelstraße
Schlesische Straße
Görlitzer Straße
Kottbusser Straße
Manteuffelstr.
Lausitzer Straße
Görlitzer Park
Reichenberger Straße
Wiener Straße
ALT-TREPTOW
Schönleinstraße
Grimmstraße
Graefestraße
Hobrechtstraße
Landwehrkanal
Ratiborstraße
Urbanstraße
Kottbusser Damm
Pflügerstraße
Lohmühlenstraße
Kiefholzstraße
LOHMÜLEN-BRÜCKE
Reuterstraße
Fichtestr.
Hasenheide
Pannierstraße
Harzer Straße
Bouchéstraße
Wildenbruchstraße
Hermannplatz
Sonnenallee
Weichselstraße
Weigandufer
Elsenstraße
Volkspark Hasenheide
Karl-Marx-Straße
WILDENBRUCH-BRÜCKE
Weserstraße
NEUKÖLLN

01.

Dennewitzstraße 2
U1, 2, 3 (Gleisdreieck)

THE UNDERGROUND HOUSE

When the underground goes through a house ...

The house located at number 2 Dennewitzstraße is a real curiosity: this old building is perhaps the only building in the world to be directly traversed (one could even say cut through) by the underground.
The (indirect) cause of this peculiarity was a serious accident on 26 September 1908, when two underground trains collided head-on in Gleisdreieck, probably due to a signalling error.
The accident claimed the lives of 18 people and left the whole town in mourning. In order to prevent such a tragedy from happening again, an alternative route was devised, but its construction was postponed in the mid-1920s due to the First World War.
At that time, the Berlin Public Transport Authority (BVG) had acquired 30 plots of land along with the

buildings on them. Instead of demolishing them, the decision was made to build new underground tracks that would cut through the houses – it was simply the cheapest solution. Most of the houses that were tunnelled through disappeared after the Battle of Berlin in 1945, but the house in Dennewitzstraße survived the war.
Since 1926, excluding the effects of air-raid warnings and driver strikes, trains on the U1 line have gone through this house 444 times a day every working day (222 times in each direction).
After crossing the park on the metal bridge, the rails of the underground train pass through a covered ramp that enters the house.
For its occupants, who have often been interviewed by the local press, it begins with a distant roar that seems to come from the bowels of the building like the depths of a mine. The noise becomes louder and turns into a roar: it sounds as if the ceilings are starting to vibrate. Rat-a-tat! The tiles on the floor echo and the noise then quickly fades away before disappearing entirely. All along this ramp, as well as in the house, the rails are enclosed in double-walled concrete casings to mitigate the unwanted noises that obviously accompany an underground train.
It must be noted that to attract occupants, rents in this house are particularly low.

02.

Stresemannstraße 66–68
S1, 2, 26, 26 (Anhalter Bahnhof)

THE TOLL WALL

The last remnants of Berlin's customs clearance wall

In the middle of Stresemannstraße, the small piece of wall which is still standing at numbers 66–68 is not the remains of a building destroyed during the last war, but the remnants of a toll wall (used for collecting customs taxes) that surrounded Berlin from the 18th to the 19th century, the partial outline of which can still be seen on Stresemannstraße, Linienstraße and Torstraße.

It was in 1987 that a section of this toll wall was reconstructed here from the original foundations.

For Frederick William I of Prussia, the 'soldier king', the city wall of Berlin (his home city and garrison town) served primarily to protect the local economy from cheap foreign products, but also to hinder smugglers who had absolutely no intention of paying the taxes due on leaving the city. It was also used to fill the coffers of the state and to stem the number of desertions within the army's ranks, as most of the Prussian troops were poorly paid, ill-treated and even kidnapped or forcibly conscripted.

The toll wall was dotted with 18 gates which were used to carry out customs controls on merchants coming into the city. Today, 17 of them are little more than a name on maps of the city.

In the 18th century, after going through the first customs control at the city's gates, the carts and wagons had to go to the Packhof (the customs warehouse) to unload their contents and pay customs on their goods.

In the days when the territory of the city went beyond the wall, this warehouse was demolished, and the customs control was moved to customs tax offices which were built well in advance of the city walls.

One of these toll barriers has been preserved: the Royal Waters Inspection pavilion on the island of Lohmühle.

A TOLL WALL WHICH AFFECTS THE LOCATION OF STATIONS

The toll wall even affected the location of the first stations, called *terminus*, where the new railways began: each of them was built outside the toll wall.

© Schlesinger

03.

Stresemannstraße 37
U1, 3, 6 (Hallesches Tor)

REMAINS OF THE STRESEMANNSTRAßE RAILWAY LINE

The railway line that once connected Berlin's train stations

At the corner of Stresemannstraße and Großbeerenstraße, on the central space separating the two pavements, there is a piece of railway line protected by railings. A sign reveals that this is a very rare relict of the first railway line that connected Berlin's train stations to each other.

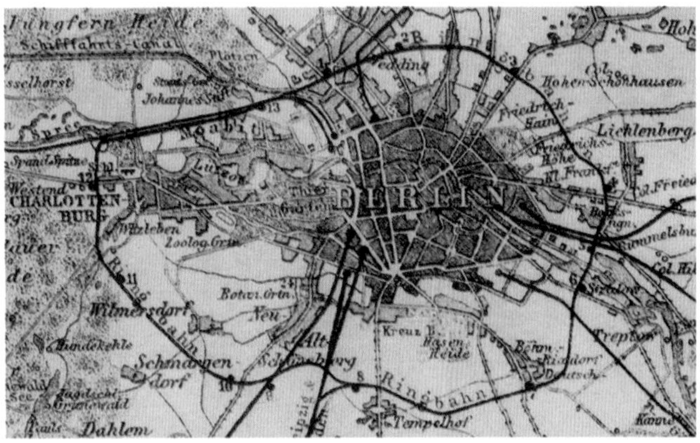

The city today is essentially a result of changes that occurred during the industrial revolution. At the beginning of the 19th century, Berlin – then the capital of Prussia – was home to a few hundred thousand inhabitants. One hundred years later, the city became the capital of the new German Empire following the political unification of Germany in 1871, and its population reached 4.5 million. As the leading industry of continental Europe, it was the third largest city in the world after New York and London. Above all, the

THE OTHER RELICT OF THE VERBINDUNGSBAHN

The passing-by of the 1851 Ring railway line is also evidenced by the name of a street in Kreuzberg that pays tribute to it: the *Eisenbahnstraße* ('road of the railway line') was the street along which the connection railway line passed as it transited between Görlitz (built subsequently in 1866-1867) and Frankfurt. In fact, where the road meets the River Spree, it lines up with the remains of the *Brommybrücke*, an old bridge whose ruins can be found at number Brommystraße 1.

© Assenmacher

arrival of the train led to the emergence of large industrial centres like Berlin, as high concentrations of production meant that raw materials could be transported to unique processing locations, and the produced goods could be quickly and affordably distributed across the country.

However, as they were so noisy and polluting, trains could not easily cross the city, which was already congested. Train stations called 'railheads' (the railway line did not cross the city and only stopped at certain Berlin stations) were initially built at the gates of the city, itself surrounded by a toll wall (*Zollmauer*, see page 64).

The railway network of the German Empire resembled a giant spider's web, at the centre of which stood Berlin. This presented a major problem: how to transfer the merchandise from one railhead to another as it transited through Berlin between opposite ends of the Empire. This was the original function of the *Ringbahn*: the S-Bahn line running around the historic centre, which was originally called the *Verbindungsbahn* (or junction line).

Redesigned during the 1860s to accommodate the growing number of stations, the current trajectory of the Ringbahn dates back to 1871. With its reduced perimeter, the first connection line, inaugurated in 1851, ensured the transit between the stations of Stettin (now the park of the northern railway station, the Nordbahnhof), Hamburg (which became the Museum of Contemporary Art in 1996), Potsdam (now the Tilla-Durieux park just by Potsdamer Platz public square), Anhalt (now the parks of Lilli-Henoch, Elise-Tilse and Gleisdreieck), and Frankfurt (later called the Silesian railway station, now the Ostbahnhof, the east railway station – the only former railhead still in use).

Since its creation, this ancestor of the Ringbahn has nearly entirely disappeared from the Berlin landscape. All that remains is the small section found on the Stresemannstraße that connected the stations of Potsdam and Anhalt.

04.

IG-Metall-Haus
Alte Jakobstraße 149
U1, 3, 6 (Hallesches Tor)

STAIRCASE OF THE GERMAN STEELWORKERS UNION

An unknown masterpiece by Erich Mendelsohn

On the corner of Alte Jakobstraße and Lindenstraße, the House of the German Steelworkers Union (IG-Metall-Haus) does not tend to capture the attention of passers-by unless they are passionate about architecture.

Accessible to the public during working hours, the building has a spectacular staircase that stretches from floor to ceiling and measures five metres in diameter. Along with its magnificent brass railing that emphasises the spiralling effect, its plunging lighting system also extends the entire height of the structure; on each floor a bunch of light bulbs is enclosed in an elegant glass sphere.

Designed by famous German architect of the time Erich Mendelsohn, briefly assisted by R.W. Reichel, the building was completed in August 1930. Its construction, which began in 1929, had been disrupted by the Great Depression of that same year, as well as a four-week strike by workers requesting more pay.

The building exhibits outstanding examples of architectural detail heralding the new Art Deco style: the gold lettering of the word 'Metall' and its typography are typical of the 1920s; the bronze finishes on the windows and the corners of some travertine walls; and the particularly unusual inwardly curved main façade.

Other notable constructions of the expressionist architect Erich Mendelsohn include the Schaubühne, an avant-garde Berlin theatre built in 1928 on Kurfürstendamm Avenue, and the spectacular Einstein Tower in Potsdam.

© Alex 1011

05.

Gitschiner Straße / Carrefour Prinzenstraße
U1, 3 (Prinzenstraße)

THE TOAD AT PRINZENSTRAßE UNDERGROUND STATION

The Toad Prince of Prussia

Coming from Kottbusser Tor underground station, at the beginning of the north platform of Prinzenstraße station, it's easy to miss the small sculpture of a toad with a golden crown on its head.

The little amphibian, who has been in the station ever since its inauguration in 1902, is a delightful little nod to three things: the name of the station (Prinzenstraße); the Frog Prince (*Der Froschkönig oder der eiserne Heinrich*) from the fairy tale by the Grimm brothers, in which a prince is transformed into a toad; and to the prince who gave his name to the street – William, Prince of Prussia.

The sculpture was created by the Royal Porcelain Manufactory KPM, which has its headquarters not far away at Wegelystraße 1, near the Tiergarten.

It has been stolen several times, but fortunately, the underground company had commissioned several copies. During the recent construction of the new glass entrance, the toad was put safely away in a cupboard; once the works were completed, it was simply forgotten. However, its absence did not go unnoticed for long.

After a complaint from several young users, the toad was given a new home in the station – in a hard to reach place to avoid further thefts.

THE STEHFISCH SCULPTURE

Wassertorstraße 65, 10969 Berlin

It is easy to miss the surprising statue in the small park on the corner of Wassertorstraße and Gitschiner Straße. The Stehfisch sculpture (which literally means 'standing fish') by Ernst Baumeister depicts a figure half-man and half-fish or half-whatever-you-want (torpedo?). It is part of a 2004 programme aimed at encouraging the development of art in public spaces.

© OTFW

06.

Bohemian-Lutheran Bethlehem Cemetery
(Böhmisch-Lutherischer Bethlehems Friedhof)
Mehringdamm 21
U6 (Mehringdamm)

GRAVE OF THE MÜHLENHAUPT FAMILY

Hats of the Resistance

The gravesite of the Mühlenhaupt family is by far the most original in the Bethlehem Cemetery in Kreuzberg. It features four stelae cast in concrete, each decorated with a colourful portrait of a member of the family: on the left, Kurt Mühlenhaupt and his wife Friedel; on the right, Kurt's siblings Wilhelm and Margarete.

The stones were made by Kurt Mühlenhaupt (1921-2006) himself, a naïve artist nicknamed the 'painter of love', who was easily recognisable by the bright red wide-brimmed hat that he never took off — it can be seen on his own gravestone. The hat originated from the deep indignation Mühlenhaupt felt as a child when a teacher hit a Jewish classmate who had the audacity to keep his school cap on as the children sang their daily national anthem. All members of the family are depicted here wearing a hat.

Along with Günter Grass, Kurt Mühlenhaupt was a member of the Berlin society of poets and painters founded in 1972 in Kreuzberg, where he lived for most of his life, not far from the cemetery where he wished to be buried. When his brother Wilhelm died in 1977, Mühlenhaupt made four stelae of precious metal, which he set with enamel portraits. In 1981 Mühlenhaupt said of them: 'For the people of Kreuzberg the cemetery is a kind of park. In order to brighten it up a bit, I have placed my own gravestone there, as well as those of my wife, sister and brother. Only my brother lies in his grave for the time being.' Stolen in the mid 1980s, the metal stelae were replaced in 1988 by the concrete ones seen there today.

Kurt
Mühlenhaupt
Maler der Liebe

07.

Dreifaltigkeitskirchhof II Cemetery
Bergmannstraße 39–41
U7 (Gneisenaustraße)

THE OPPENFELD FAMILY MAUSOLEUM

A striking Egyptian-style mausoleum

Built in 1828 for Georg Moritz and Carl Daniel Oppenfeld, members of the Berlin banking family of the same name, an Egyptian-style mausoleum regularly surprises walkers who venture into the eastern part of the Dreifaltigkeitskirchhof II cemetery.

The reason why the Oppenfelds chose this particular style is unknown. Perhaps it was simply to follow the Egyptian fashion that swept across Europe in the 19th century following Napoleon Bonaparte's Egyptian campaign between 1798 and 1801? Or because the Oppenfelds were Freemasons, for whom ancient Egypt and its mystery schools held an important place?

One thing is certain: although it might be tempting to think so, this choice has nothing to do with the famous Egyptologist and writer Georg Ebers, the son of a cousin of Georg Moritz Oppenfeld: Ebers was born in 1837, nine years after the mausoleum was built.

The Oppenheim family had obtained permission to change their name to Oppenfeld in 1827, just before the mausoleum was built: Georg Moritz had renounced the Jewish faith and converted to Catholicism in 1822, thereby relinquishing his Jewish first name, Moses.

OTHER EGYPTIAN-STYLE MAUSOLEUMS

In the Dorotheenstadt cemetery (Chausseestraße 126) stands the Liman family mausoleum, also in the Egyptian style. In 1820, the architect Ludwig Liman had taken part in the expedition led by the German general von Minutoli, and died in Alexandria that same year. In the Sophien II Cemetery (Bergstraße 29), the Koehne family tomb also features a truncated pyramid structure.

v. OPPENFELD'S ERBBEGRAEBNISS.
1828.

08.

Luisenstadt Cemetery
Lot 10 – in the middle of the east side (left as you enter)
Südstern 8–12
U7 (Südstern)

TOMB OF ERWIN REIBEDANZ

An astonishing expressionist comet

In the Luisenstadt Cemetery, the grave of businessman Erwin Reibedanz (1878-1919) is one of the strangest in Berlin. It depicts a comet knocking over a cross as it rises from the ground. The comet is carved out of a limestone called *Muschelkalk* (shell limestone), and constitutes a spiked ball that has a long rectangular tail adorned with rays trailing behind it.

Although it now looks rather dull, it was originally a bright polychrome work of art; surrounded by a hedge of red roses, the base and the cross were painted in dark blue-grey and the lower part of the tail was an intense blue, while the star and the reliefs of the rays were golden. As soon as it was unveiled it was met with strong protests that quickly got the better of this wild array of colours.

Some see in this work an expression of Christian belief, with the comet being the triumphant spirit of death, itself represented by the cross that it tips over. However, it is more likely that the sculpture is a reference to Halley's Comet, which shocked the world when it passed by a few years earlier in April 1910. Reibedanz, who was close to the most avant-garde architects of his time, commissioned the comet in the expressionist style from Max Taut, a pioneer of expressionist architecture and the brother of the famous modern architect Bruno Taut.

There were fears that Halley's Comet – the leitmotif of the expressionist worldview – would annihilate all life on Earth by enveloping it in a cloud of poisonous gas. In this regard, the tombstone would therefore celebrate the overthrow of religion through the passage of the comet.

WHAT IS EXPRESSIONISM?

Expressionism appeared at the beginning of the 20th century in Northern Europe, particularly in Germany, and is an artistic current that spanned many fields: painting, architecture, literature, theatre, cinema, music, dance, etc. Condemned by the Nazi regime as 'degenerate art', expressionism tends to distort reality in order to inspire an emotional reaction in the viewer. Representations are often based on anguished visions and reflect the pessimistic view that expressionists had of their time, which was threatened by the First World War, itself heralded by the passage of Halley's Comet in 1910. As photographic techniques improved and the relationship between art and reality was profoundly modified, expressionism also broke with impressionism (which described physical reality) in a rather aggressive manner through the use of vivid colours and sharp lines. Expressionism is not really a movement or a school, but rather a reaction against academism and society. *Der Blaue Reiter* ('The Blue Rider') and *Die Brücke* ('The Bridge') are the two best known groups of expressionist-inspired artists. 'The Scream' by painter Edvard Munch and Franz Marc's 'The Blue Horse' are two of the most famous paintings of this genre. In music, Dmitri Shostakovich's symphonies were expressionist in spirit from the late 1920s onwards.

09.

Reichenberger Straße 140–151
U1, U3 (Görlitzer Bahnhof)

ART INSTALLATIONS ON REICHENBERGER STRAßE

In memory of the district's industrial past

On the corner of Reichenbergerstraße and Manteuffelstraße in Kreuzberg, the mindful passer-by will notice that incorporated in the pavement's paving stones is a piece of railway a few metres long in which a series of horseshoes are arranged. Further down Reichenbergerstraße going east, several mosaics and 16 cement slabs, in which various tools and mechanical parts have been cast, are visible among the stone slabs.

These installations were made after the fall of the Berlin Wall at the beginning of the 1990s and are the fruits of an artistic project begun in the 1980s. As part of the 1986 International Building Exhibition Berlin (IBA), the Kreuzberg district city hall organised a competition aimed at improving the image of this street – given its notorious filthiness – by recalling its glorious pre-war past.

Following the political division of Germany and the creation of West Berlin, the western part lost its status as capital and became a rather poor city full of artists, baby boomers and rebels. Surrounded by the Wall on three sides, the famous SO36 (South West 36, a district named after the postal codes of West Berlin introduced after the construction of the Wall), the part of Kreuzberg located north of the Landwehr Canal, became the dodgiest area in Berlin, full of squats. In contrast, district 61 in the other part of Kreuzberg was deemed bourgeois. As the saying went: *36 brennt, 61 pennt* – '36 burns, 61 sleeps'.

Until the Second World War, this was a vibrant working-class neighbourhood in continental Europe's most populous and industrialised country. For example, Carl

Lindström (Schlesischestraße 26) became Europe's number one manufacturer of records and gramophones. In this regard, Reichenbergerstraße was a typical road. Of the 15 art installations that were apparently intended to grace the wide pavements, at least 10 were completed, some of which are now unfortunately in a poor state or even unrecognisable.

Follow the instructions below to find them:

– In front of Reichenbergerstraße 153, not far from Manteufelstraße and on the north side, is a partly damaged mosaic of an unclear subject made by an unknown artist.

– On the corner of Reichenbergerstraße and Manteufelstraße, on the north side, horseshoes and rails are visible. They are a reminder that until the electrification of train lines around the end of the 19th century, a horse-drawn tramway passed by here. On the south side is another mosaic by an unknown artist. Again, the subject is unclear due to its deteriorated state.

– On Reichenbergerstraße, between Manteufelstraße and Lausitzer-straße, on the north side, metallic tools have been cast in the 16 cement slabs. They refer to the various workshops and factories that once occupied the courtyards.

– On the corner of Reichenbergerstraße and Lausitzerstraße, on the north side, is yet another anonymous mosaic that seems to resemble a knight in armor accompanied by a dove. This work symbolises the Saint Mary hospice located at Lausitzerstraße 44, founded at the beginning of the 20th century by catholic nuns of the congregation of Saint Mary of the Immaculate Conception.

– On the corner of Reichenbergerstraße and Lausitzerstraße, on the south side, is a mosaic by Lutz Werner Brandt entitled *Vom Milchgeschäft zum Supermarkt* – meaning 'From Creamery to Supermarket'. It depicts a bar code surrounded by four old-fashioned signs displaying the words *Milch*, *Brot*, *Butter*, and *Käse* – milk, bread, butter, and cheese. The work refers to the not-so-distant past, before supermarkets had invaded our neighbourhoods and forced specialist shops to close.

– In front of number 64-66 on the south side of Reichenbergerstraße is an anonymous mosaic of a collapsing chimney crashing through a blue sky with a rainbow. In the spring of 1977 a group of citizens occupied the former red brick firehouse located at Reichenbergerstraße 66; they wanted to turn it into a community centre. However, the building and its big chimney were demolished by the city on 12 May 1977, shattering the dreams of those who had occupied it.

– On the corner of Reichenbergerstraße and Ohlauerstraße, on the north side in front of number 126, is a mosaic by Irene Niepel. It depicts piano keys and refers to the famous Bechstein pianos. The premises in which the pianos were produced are still visible today at Ohlauerstraße 5-11 and Reichenbergerstraße 124. With an annual production of 5,000 pianos, Bechstein was the world's leading piano producer at the beginning of the 20th century.

– In front of numbers 101 and 90 on the north and south sides of Reichenbergerstraße are mosaics of snakes, the symbolism of which is unknown, as is the artist.

– In front of Reichenbergerstraße 80 is a beautiful mosaic by Lutz Werner Brandt showing a telephone handset surrounded by wires. The work pays tribute to the company Richard Bosse and Co., located at Wienerstraße 43, one street north of Reichenbergerstraße. During the 20th century, the company proved to be a major player in the telephone industry before it was bought by AGFEO in 1978.

10.

Adalbertstraße 79 and Waldemarstraße 46
U1, 3, 8 (Kottbusser Tor)

RELIEFS ON THE FAÇADE OF ADALBERTSTRAßE 79

A building that was 'de-stuccoed' then redecorated

At the corner of Adalbertstrasse and Waldemarstrasse is a building dating from the Industrial Revolution; its smooth façades are enhanced with reliefs and painted motifs.

STUCCO FROM BERLIN'S FAÇADES WAS REMOVED

Until the Second World War, the façades of buildings in Berlin were over-embellished. In the industrial megalopolis suffering from unimaginable social inequalities, this exuberance displayed the pomp of the rich as much as it concealed the misery of the working class. Austrian architect Alfred Loos was the first to denounce this love of artifice and the need to display so-called superiority through external signs. This was the birth of modern architecture, which set out to fight ostentation and lies. Post-war Germany was rebuilt with ruthless pragmatism. Entire districts that had survived the bombing were demolished to make way for the modern city. Of the 1.5 million dwellings from the late 19th or early 20th century still inhabited in post-war Berlin, only a third are still standing. Half of them have had the stucco of their façades removed to bring them up to date. Between 1920 and 1979, 1,400 buildings in Kreuzberg alone were de-stuccoed. Legend has it that the Berlin de-stuccoers were even paid by the kilo. It was not until the late 1960s that voices began to be raised in favour of the preservation of this architectural heritage. In West Berlin, investments were first made in the renovation of certain streets that were particularly representative of the Wilhelmian era: Planufer and Chamissoplatz in Kreuzberg, Reformationsplatz in Spandau, and Schloßstrasse and Christstrasse in Charlottenburg were the first to find favour with the authorities. In the east it was much later, on the occasion of the 750th anniversary of the city in 1987, that the idea was born to turn the districts of Kollwitz and Helmholz on Prenzlauer Berg into a kind of open-air museum in memory of what the working-class areas of Berlin used to be like. Today, there are neighbouring buildings all over Berlin, some of which have been deprived of their stucco, and others that have not. In Kreuzberg, for example, heading to Planufer from the Admiralbrücke, you can walk along the Landwehrkanal and admire the opulence of the many ornate façades ... until you reach number 96, where the charm comes to a sudden halt. Unlike its neighbours, it was the target of the prevailing policy in post-war Germany to remove stucco. Another example is in Prenzlauer Berg: at the corner of Esmarchstrasse and Käthe-Niederkirchnerstrasse there are two identical buildings facing each other that date back to 1903. While it appears that the stucco of one has been removed, the other has not suffered the same fate. And the difference is rather spectacular.

Between the windows on the ground and first floors is a string of ceramic figures depicting scenes of children playing in a park; they are doing somersaults, running, playing tug-of-war, hopscotch ... One child watches his balloon take off a few floors up. The cornices of the roof are covered with friezes and medallions representing various characters, including a naked woman. The windows are highlighted with a fine line of colour drawn with a brush. Some, which appear to be chosen randomly, are more lavishly decorated and set with enamels. They are reminiscent of the German architect Hundertwasser's 'window right', which urged inhabitants to embellish the space around their windows 'as far as the arm could reach'. These listed decorations are the work of Yater Hanefi, an artist of Turkish origin who received part of his education at the Academy of Art in Berlin (West) during the Cold War. He created these facades in 1984 as part of the International Architecture Exhibition (*Internationale Bauausstellung*, IBA), a federal institution aimed at promoting the urban, social and ecological development of German cities. It is perhaps surprising that the building, which dates back to 1864-1866, does not have the typical Neo-Baroque facades of the time. They were in fact 'de-stuccoed' from 1920 onwards following the advent of modern architecture in Germany (see opposite).

11.

Kunstquartier Bethanien
Mariannenplatz 2
U1, 3, 8 (Kottbusser Tor)

THE FAÇADE OF THE BETHANIE

A building inspired by the Ducal Palace of Urbino, Italy

On Mariannenplatz in Kreuzberg, the Bethanien is a famous arts centre in Berlin. But what few Berliners know is that this former deaconess hospital, built between 1845 and 1847 to plans by Ludwig Persius – court architect and pupil of the famous Karl Friedrich Schinkel – is said to have been largely inspired by the Ducal Palace of Urbino in Italy.
In particular, the *torricini* ('small towers') of the Italian Renaissance building, which share an identical structure with the two towers of the Bethanie.
Some also suggest that Frederick William IV (1795–1861), a connoisseur of architecture and great admirer of the Italian Renaissance, may himself have suggested the Italian model.

Persius designed other buildings inspired by Italy: the Friedenskirche (Church of Peace) in the park of Sanssouci Palace in Potsdam (see the guide *Secret Potsdam* from the same publisher) takes its form from the Basilica of San Clemente in Rome, based on sketches drawn by Frederick William IV himself.

© Jörg Zägel

© Sailko

12.

Kunstquartier Bethanien
Mariannenplatz 2
U1, 3, 8 (Kottbusser Tor)

THEODOR FONTANE'S PHARMACY

A journey through time

Located within the Bethanien Art Center (see page 84), in the right wing of the ground floor, the Theodor-Fontane-Apotheke (Theodor Fontane Pharmacy), the hospital's former pharmacy, is one of Berlin's best-kept secrets.

With its original woodwork and various period containers and bottles, the pharmacy, built in 1848–49, is one of the most beautiful historic pharmacies in Germany.

It was here that the famous writer Theodor Fontane (1819–1898), one of the leading German representatives of realism in literature, worked for a time as a pharmacist.

Theodor Fontane was in fact the son of the pharmacist Louis Henry Fontane (1796–1867) and Émilie Fontane (1797–1869), both descendants of Huguenots.

Upon arriving in Berlin in 1845, Theodor, following in his parents' footsteps, first worked at Dr. Julius Eduard Schacht's Polish pharmacy before obtaining his pharmacist's license in 1847 and being hired at Bethania, which had just opened its doors. He remained there for two years, during which time he also trained the first two women in Berlin to learn this trade, which had until then been reserved exclusively for men.

It was immediately after his time at Bethania that Fontane abandoned his career as a pharmacist to devote himself full-time to writing and journalism, while actively participating in the March 1848 revolutionary uprisings, fighting for German national unity against the monarchical regime.

In his autobiography *Von Zwanzig bis Dreißig* ('From Twenty to Thirty'), Fontane recounts, among other things, his two years at Bethania and his meeting with Emmy Danckwerts, one of the two deaconesses he had trained and whom he admired for her intelligence, strength of character, and kindness of heart.

The hospital's former pharmacy is managed by the Friedrichshain-Kreuzberg Museum (Adalbertstraße 95a), a museum dedicated to preserving the history of the Kreuzberg and Friedrichshain neighborhoods.

As a plaque at No. 3 Mariannenplatz, near one of the building's entrances, notes, Fontane lived within Bethania.

13.

Köpenicker Straße 8
U1, U3 (Schlesisches Tor)

THE TWO-WHEELER MUSEUM

The charm of old Berlin

You do not stumble upon the Two-Wheeler Museum (Zweiradmuseum) by chance. Near the Oberbaum Bridge, at 8 Köpenicker Strasse, you must first ring the intercom before entering a charming inner courtyard that opens directly onto the Spree.

Founded in 1987 by Stefan Klinkenberg, a collector and restorer of vintage motorcycles, the museum houses a collection of around 30 vehicles, mainly dating from the 1920s to the 1960s.

Visitors can admire motorcycles, bicycles, mopeds and sidecars, including major German brands such as BMW, NSU and Horex, as well as a few rare models from England and Russia, alongside old posters, signs and advertisements.

Run by a team of enthusiasts, the venue is not merely a museum; it is also a working workshop where machines are restored and sometimes even rebuilt using period parts.

NSU
MOTORRÄDER
SPORTMODELLE
NECKARSULMER FAHRZEUGWERKE A.G. NECKARSULM
MOTOR OEL

NEUKÖLLN

01. THE FORGOTTEN SYMBOLS OF THE IDEAL-PASSAGE *p. 92*

02. THE STONES OF ALFRED-SCHOLZ-PLATZ *p. 94*

03. CAFÉ BOTANICO GARDEN *p. 96*

04. SRI MAYURAPATHY MURUGAN HINDU TEMPLE *p. 98*

01.

Fuldastraße 55–56D / Weichselstraße 8–8F
U7 (Rathaus-Neukölln)

THE FORGOTTEN SYMBOLS OF THE IDEAL-PASSAGE

Inspired by the opera *Der Freischütz*

Built in 1907/08 by the architects Paul and Willi Kind for a cooperative formed by employees from the health insurance company Allgemeine Ortskrankenkasse (AOK), the Ideal-Passage (listed in 1998), linking Fuldastraße and Weichselstraße by means of three inner courtyards, is not a complete secret to the inhabitants of the area. But few realize that the complex, which became a model of social housing at the time of its construction, was built following the structure of the opera *Der Freischütz* (*The Marksman*), as commemorated by a plaque on both entrances.
Each courtyard has therefore been designed with reference to a scene from the opera.
The first one, near Fuldastraße, boasting an animal above every doorway, represents the 'Festplatz des Dorfes', the village fairground landscaped with hedging and hornbeam thorn. In 2006, the courtyard additionally acquired the 'Belles Poules', metal sculptures by the German-French artists Gabriele Roßkamp and Serge Petit. A statue of the hunter, Max, used to be in the yard depicting the 'Waldhof' (forest clearing).
The second courtyard with its façade paintings of a fountain, a cock, a duck and a farmer and his wife, was destroyed during World War II, as was one of the buildings and parts of a side wing of Weichselstraße. It represented a rural village ('bäuerliches Dorf').
The third and last courtyard corresponds to the 'Wolfsschlucht', the wolf's glen, Samiel's hiding place: some façade adornments represent the wild animals and spirits which appeared while Kaspar was casting the bullets.

DER FREISCHÜTZ

Composed in 1821 by Carl Maria von Weber and considered the first romantic opera in Germany, *Der Freischütz* tells the story of the huntsman's apprentice, Max, and Agathe, his fiancée and daughter of the hereditary forester. Both have to fight for their love against Kaspar, who is assisted by Samiel.

55c

02.

Alfred Scholz Platz, Karl-Marx-Straße 111
U7 (Rathaus-Neukölln)

THE STONES OF ALFRED-SCHOLZ-PLATZ

Mosaic of diversity

Most people who pass through the busy Alfred-Scholz-Platz every day do not even notice that this square is not like others: if you look carefully, you will notice that along Karl-Marx-Straße, some stones have been assembled along a line with inscriptions consisting of a name, a region of origin, and a percentage that corresponds to the percentage of residents in Neukölln who come from that region.

The square is also partly composed of coloured stones: 67.8% of these stones in the square are greywacke corresponding to the German residents, 13.6% are basalt representing immigrants from the Middle East, 9% are granite for those who came from Eastern Europe, and so on.

Across the square, some stones are marked with a discreet cross that commemorates those who actively joined the project and repaved the square.

Called 'Meinstein' ('My Stone'), the mosaic was created by the artist Nadia Kaabi-Linke and represents the very diverse population of northern Neukölln.

From 2010 to 2014, the Tunisian-born artist worked together with the architectural firm el:ch Landschaftsarchitekten on the 910 square metres, placing about 150,000 stones from all over the world.

During meetings conducted by the Dutch artist Roos Versteeg in 2011, Neuköllners discussed homeland, immigration and shared their impressions regarding memory, hope, longing, anger, fear and happiness.

This information was translated into a code designed by the Berlin media artist Ralf Baecker, and later became the graphic image used for the Meinstein plan.

Formerly called Platz der Stadt Hof, the square was reopened in April 2014 and renamed after Alfred Scholz, the first SPD mayor in Neukölln, elected in 1919.

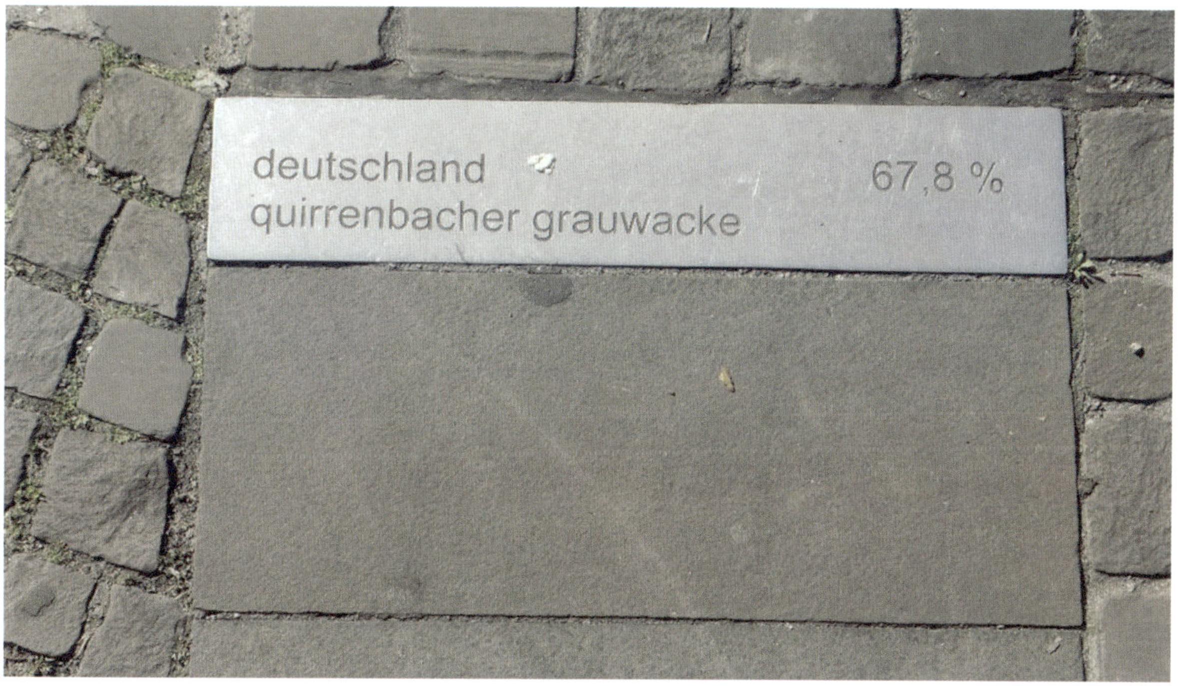
deutschland
67,8 %
quirrenbacher grauwacke

03.

Richardstraße 100
U7 (Rathaus-Neukölln)

CAFÉ BOTANICO GARDEN

A secret permaculture garden

From the street, there is nothing to indicate that Café Botanico is more than a café: step inside, go through the restaurant to the inner courtyard, keep going and take the small path on the left that follows a private garden on the right.

After about 100 metres, you will discover a fantastic, large permaculture garden (1000 square metres) that boasts an assortment of 200 plants, two-thirds being edible, from the exotic paracress to the familiar apple tree.

This wild garden was established in 2012 by Martin Höfft, using permaculture methods of cultivation and Masanobu Fukuoka's natural farming philosophy. The soil is fertilised by compost and plant manure made from nettle, comfrey, cabbage leaves, yaw, horsetail and other vegetable remains. Martin avoids digging and tilling, working the soil only on the surface. Chemical pesticides are completely banned. The plants should grow as freely as possible in a living and self-regulating space that welcomes bees and butterflies – a bee colony is also part of this ecosystem.

Once a month, Martin guides a group of eight people through his crops. During a one-hour tour, he explains what permaculture is and how he approaches it, tells the story of his garden and presents the best of his wild herbs, the garden's highlight.

Most of the ingredients of the café come, of course, from the garden.

04.

Blaschkoallee 48/Riesestraße 20–22
U7 (Blaschkoallee)

SRI MAYURAPATHY MURUGAN HINDU TEMPLE

Object of veneration

The brightly coloured Sri Mayurapathy Murugan temple with its red and white stripes stands out in stark contrast in the middle of the rather banal buildings of the Blaschkoallee and the Riesestraße.

Two rainbow-coloured towers (*gorupas*) rise five or seven metres high over them and are home to a wide range of Hindu gods.

Inside the centre of this Hindu temple dedicated to Shiva, various other colourful gods are venerated. The main god in the temple is Murugan, one of Shiva's sons, just like Ganesh.

Built between 2009 and 2013 by the Indian architect Govindan Ravi Shankar, the Murugan temple is connected to the Tamils from Sri Lanka who came to Berlin in the 1980s at the outbreak of the civil war in their country.

Today, there are more than 1,100 of them living in Berlin and they have recreated their country's spiritual environment in Neukölln.

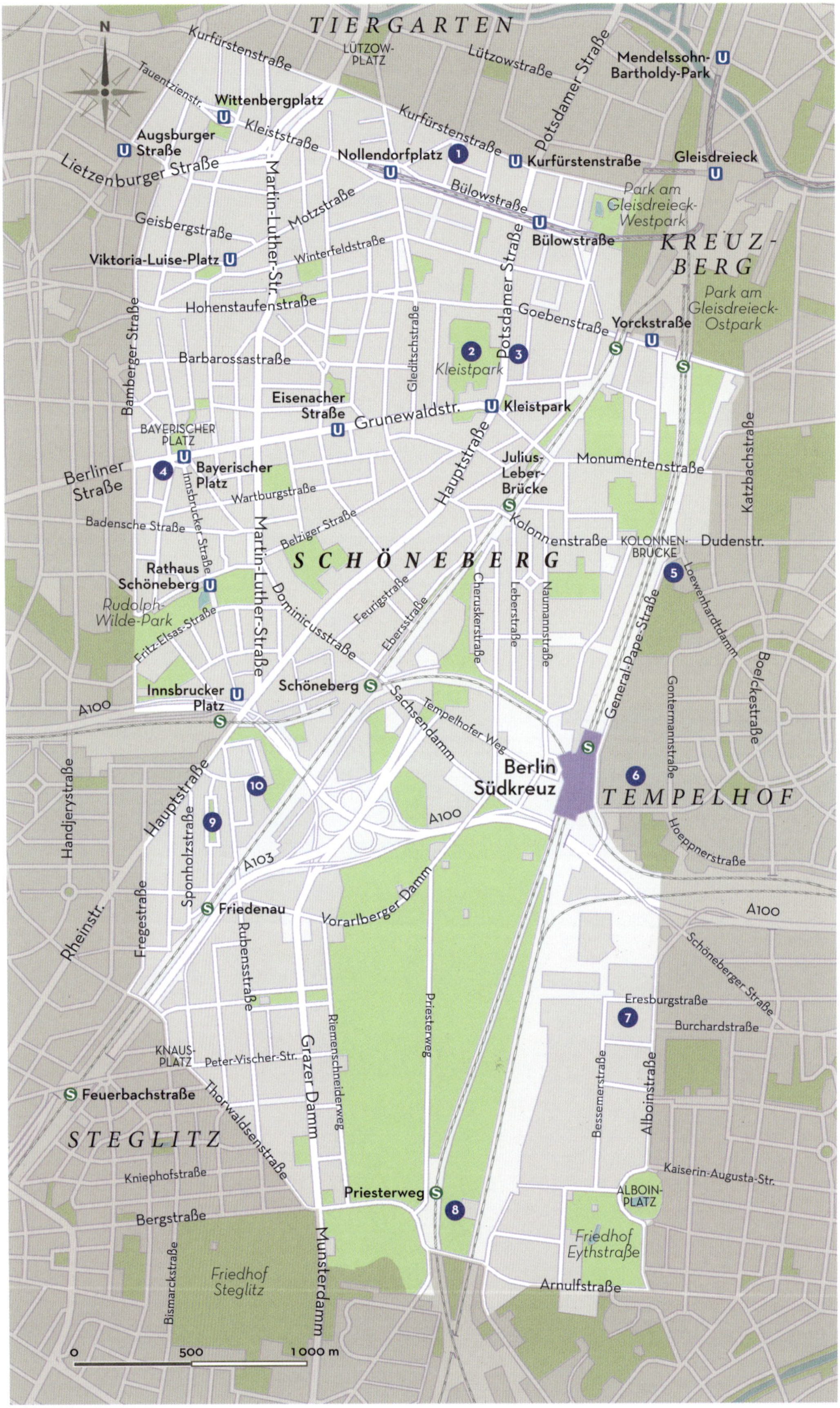
N
TIERGARTEN
LÜTZOW-PLATZ
Kurfürstenstraße
Lützowstraße
Potsdamer Straße
Mendelssohn-Bartholdy-Park
Tauentzienstr.
Wittenbergplatz
Augsburger Straße
Kleiststraße
Nollendorfplatz
1
Kurfürstenstraße
Gleisdreieck
Lietzenburger Straße
Bülowstraße
Park am Gleisdreieck-Westpark
Geisbergstraße
Motzstraße
Martin-Luther-Str.
Bülowstraße
KREUZ-BERG
Viktoria-Luise-Platz
Winterfeldstraße
Park am Gleisdreieck-Ostpark
Hohenstaufenstraße
Goebenstraße
Yorckstraße
Bamberger Straße
Gleditschstraße
2
3
Barbarossastraße
Kleistpark
Eisenacher Straße
Grunewaldstr.
Kleistpark
BAYERISCHER PLATZ
Katzbachstraße
Berliner Straße
4
Bayerischer Platz
Hauptstraße
Julius-Leber-Brücke
Monumentenstraße
Innsbrucker Straße
Wartburgstraße
Badensche Straße
Belziger Straße
Kolonnenstraße
KOLONNEN-BRÜCKE
Dudenstr.
SCHÖNEBERG
Rathaus Schöneberg
Martin-Luther-Straße
Dominicusstraße
Cheruskerstraße
Leberstraße
Naumannstraße
5
Loewenhardtdamm
Rudolph-Wilde-Park
Fritz-Elsas-Straße
Feurigstraße
Ebersstraße
General-Pape-Straße
Boelckestraße
Gontermannstraße
Innsbrucker Platz
Schöneberg
Sachsendamm
Tempelhofer Weg
A100
Berlin Südkreuz
6
TEMPELHOF
Handjerystraße
Hauptstraße
10
9
A100
Sponholzstraße
Hoeppnerstraße
A103
Rheinstr.
Fregestraße
Friedenau
Vorarlberger Damm
A100
Rubensstraße
Schöneberger Straße
Priesterweg
Eresburgstraße
7
Burchardstraße
KNAUS-PLATZ
Peter-Vischer-Str.
Riemenschneiderweg
Grazer Damm
Bessemerstraße
Alboinstraße
Feuerbachstraße
Thorwaldsenstraße
STEGLITZ
Kaiserin-Augusta-Str.
Kniephofstraße
Priesterweg
8
ALBOIN-PLATZ
Bergstraße
Friedhof Eythstraße
Bismarckstraße
Friedhof Steglitz
Munsterdamm
Arnulfstraße
0
500
1000 m

SCHÖNEBERG

01.

An der Apostelkirche 1
U1, 2, 3, 4 (Nollendorfplatz)

WINDOWS OF THE CHURCH OF THE TWELVE APOSTLES

Windows made of thousands of liquor bottles

Inaugurated in 1874, the Zwölf-Apostel-Kirche (Church of the Twelve Apostles) does not initially stand out from other churches built in similar Neo-Gothic style. Yet walking around the outside, it becomes clear that some of the windows are not simple panes or stained glass; they are actually made from the bottoms of more than 50,000 gin bottles.
Berlin was the most heavily bombed city of the Second World War. Official figures vary greatly, but according to some estimates, the total weight of all the bombs dropped on Berlin amounts to 450,000 tonnes. Assuming that the average bomb weighed 250 kilos, this would represent about 2 million bombs.
Unsurprisingly, Berlin suffered from a shortage of windows in the post-war period; to replace the windows of the city's various churches, the city had to make do with what it could find. So, as early as the spring of 1945, the local religious community undertook to renovate the Church of the Twelve Apostles, which had been badly damaged in the bombings of 22-23 November 1943.
The family that owned the GILKA spirits company came up with a truly novel idea, and generously offered thousands of bottles to help rebuild the gigantic windows that had been destroyed.
Renovated in 2018-19 thanks to a federal grant of 28,000, these extraordinary windows are now classified as historic monuments.

02.

Elßholzstraße 30–33
U7 (Kleistpark)

BERLIN COURT OF APPEALS

An architectural gem open to the public

Built between 1909 and 1913 by Rudolf Mönnich and Paul Thoemer, the Kammergericht (Court of Appeal) is surprisingly little known to Berliners, let alone tourists, as visits are quite limited: the plenary hall is only open to the public on the first Thursday of the month, from 3.30pm to 5.30pm.

It is, however, an architectural gem, featuring frescoes by the German painter Albert Maennchen and a balcony above the fireplace that was specifically designed to allow the emperor to physically tower over the crowd.

Also note the imposing circular hall at the entrance and a series of gilded medallions near the top floor: they depict historical figures associated with justice. Among them are Solon, Hammurabi, Solomon, and Aristotle.

Next to the main staircase, you can also see a wooden bulletin board used after the war by the Allied Control Council (*Alliierter Kontrollrat*): this body, which had its headquarters in the current building until 1948, posted its meeting schedule there.

THE PERMANENT SEAT OF THE INTERNATIONAL MILITARY TRIBUNAL THAT TRIED WAR CRIMINALS AT THE NUREMBERG TRIALS

On October 18, 1945, the International Military Tribunal that tried war criminals at the Nuremberg Trials convened for the first time in the Plenarsaal.

Although it is no longer in its original building, the Kammergericht (Court of Appeal) is the oldest court in Germany still in operation: it was founded in 1468 by Frederick II of Brandenburg.

© Ansgar Koreng

03.

Steinmetzstraße 22
U2, 3 (Bülowstraße)

MOSAIC OF A COW

The memory of the last Schöneberg milk house

It is a kind of tradition in Berlin – or at least common practice – to inscribe the history of the city onto its wide pavements. The installations on Reichenbergerstraße in the district of Kreuzberg (see page 78), or more recently of Gunter Demnig's famous *Stolpersteine*, are a good example of this.

In front of Steinmetzstraße 22 in the Schöneberg district a section of grey paving has been replaced by a colourful mosaic of a friendly-looking spotted cow with a swollen udder. The mosaic is a reminder that until 1982 the inner courtyard of the building was home to the 31 cows of Milchhof Mendler, the last milk house in the inner city – Berliners call the part of Berlin inside the Ringbahn the *Innenstadt*, meaning 'city centre'. The first courtyard was a shed that served as a point of sale from where more than 80,000 litres of milk were distributed every year. As for the cowshed, it was located in the second courtyard. To complete the menagerie, pigs, chickens and rabbits were raised in the cellars.

The farm was then relocated to Rudow; until 1996 it had 80 dairy cows, 300 breeding pigs, and 30 hectares of cultivated land. Today, the farm has been converted into a horse riding school with 65 hectares of land still dedicated to corn and pasture.

A UNIQUE EXAMPLE OF URBAN BIODIVERSITY IN EUROPE

With 2,500 public parks, 48% green space, 53 mammal species, a bird sanctuary (180 bird species are represented in Berlin, more than in the whole of Brandenburg), and 20,000 plant species, Berlin is a unique example of urban biodiversity in Europe.

In 2018 the German capital, whose 1,900 hectares (19 square kilometres) of land are still farmed by 41 farmers, officially had more than 1,200 farm animals, despite the fact that farming activity now takes place exclusively on the outskirts of the city. In 1928 there were about 25,000 dairy cows in Berlin, crowded into the inner courtyards of workers' housing areas in the heart of the capital. At the beginning of the 20th century, virtually every street in the inner city had at least one cowshed supplying the neighbourhood with butter, cheese, and fresh milk seven days a week. By the end of the 1920s, these barns alone covered about 17% of the city's dairy needs ... with all the associated inconveniences: smell, noise, and unhygienic conditions. Until the early 1980s, the incongruity of these urban milk houses in West Berlin was prolonged by the presence of the Wall; Berliners of Turkish origin were particularly pleased as it meant they were still able to find the fresh unpasteurised milk that allowed them to make delicious yoghurt.

04.

Streets around Bayerischer Platz
U4, 7 (Bayerischer Platz)

ORTE DES ERINNERNS MEMORIAL

A memorial for the neighbourhood

Discreetly placed to the right of the entrance to Schöneberg Town Hall is a map pinpointing several locations around Bayerischer Platz, just a few minutes' walk away.

These points highlight a series of 80 street signs that recall anti-Semitic laws of the 1930s. One side of each sign displays text and the date on which the corresponding law was enacted; on the other side is a pictogram related to the text. The signs are a spectacular symbol of remembrance.

In 1933 there were 16,000 Jews living in this district of Schöneberg, which was then called the Bayerisches Viertel (Bavarian Quarter) because of the architecture of its bourgeois buildings. Among the residents were the physicist Albert Einstein, political scientist Hannah Arendt, writer Gertrud Kolmar, and photographer Helmut Newton. More than 6,000 Jews from this district were murdered by the Nazis after Hitler came to power.

Schöneberg was one of the first districts of Berlin to take the initiative to honour a duty of remembrance, ensuring that its lost inhabitants were not forgotten.

Designed by artists Renata Stih and Frieder Schnock, the Orte des Erinnerns (Places of Memory) memorial was inaugurated in 1993.

In order to strengthen the link to the past, certain signs are sited in symbolic locations; for example, the sign declaring 'Aryan and non-Aryan children are not allowed to play together' appears next to a playground (opposite Heilbronner Straße 14) once visited by families in the neighbourhood.

SOME EXAMPLES OF SIGNS

Jews are not permitted to leave their apartments after 8pm (9pm during the summer). September 1, 1939

Costs for treatment by a Jewish doctor after April 1, 1933 will not be reimbursed by the City of Berlin's public health insurance company. March 31, 1933

Jews are no longer allowed to have household pets. February 15, 1942

Two other maps showing the locations of the 80 signs are located at the south-east corner of Bayerischer Platz and on Münchener Straße, just south of the intersection with Hohenstaufenstraße.

The smartphone application 'Orte des Erinnerns' is available to translate versions of the texts to visitors who do not speak German.

05.

General-Pape-Straße 100, Tor 1
S1, 26 (Julius-Leber-Brücke)

THE SCHWERBELASTUNGSKÖRPER

A huge concrete cylinder that measured subsidence for the Germania project

Hidden away from the street behind trees on General-Pape-Straße is an astonishing and spectacular secret place: the Schwerbelastungskörper (literally 'heavy load structure') is a large concrete cylinder weighing 12,650 tonnes and measuring 21 metres in diameter by 14 metres high.

Hitler's monumental Arc de Triomphe – which was part of the Germania project (see next double page) – was supposed to be erected just a few metres away and last an eternity: the 170 metre-wide arch was called the 'T structure' by the Nazis and stood 117 metres high, over twice the height and 20 times the weight of the Arc de Triomphe in Paris. The names of all the German soldiers who had fallen during the First World War were to be engraved on its façades – all 1.8 million of them.

Hitler hated Berlin and did not hesitate to destroy whole sections of it, but he feared that the city's ground – made of till, a mixture of rocky sediment and unstratified loose material left behind by glaciers – would collapse under the colossal weight of the arch. The Schwerbelastungskörper was used to test (down to a depth of 17 metres) the capacity of the ground to support the expected weight of the monumental arch. To do this, an optical device located inside the structure measured how fast the concrete cylinder was sinking into the till.

Designed in 1941 by Albert Speer, the building ultimately went unused. But unlike the many colossal constructions that were planned but never built by the Nazis, this concrete mastodon is undeniably real, and has been listed as a protected building since 1995.

In the two and half years following 1941, the Schwerblastungskörper sank 19.3 cm instead of the required 2 cm maximum limit.

© Dieter Brügmann

© Furfur

GERMANIA, HITLER AND ALBERT SPEER'S CRAZY PROJECT FOR THE 'WORLD CAPITAL'

After having failed the entrance exam to the Vienna Academy of Fine Arts twice, Adolf Hitler was convinced that he was an unrecognised artist. To earn a living, he sold watercolour sketches of Vienna. After having been temporarily blinded in the First World War, he decided to launch into politics after he was cured in 1920. At this time, he was already obsessed by the idea of a Great German Reich and was sure that even a thousand years after the fall of this empire, its greatness would be measured by what it would leave behind.
Hitler developed the idea of two flagship buildings in the architectural sketches he drew in 1925 – these buildings would be in the capital of his imaginary Great Reich that he called 'Germania' and constituted a triumphal arch and a grand people's hall for assemblies.
After his accession to power, Hitler's architectural ramblings began to take form during discussions with Albert Speer, a fervent Nazi and freshly qualified architect, whom the dictator promoted to the rank of Inspector General of Construction for the capital of the Reich.
In 1937, after having received Hitler's approval, Speer's partly illustrated plans for Berlin/Germania were published in the press. On 4 October, the new law on the reconstruction of German towns constituted the legal basis that was to allow the grand scale demolition of existing districts to make way for new buildings situated in strategic areas of the city centre. The published plans made absolutely no reference to the 'world capital Germania'. Hitler simply referred to 'Germania' or to the restructuration of the capital of the Reich. The prestigious buildings imagined by Hitler (the Great Dome/Hall of the People and the Triumphal Arch) are only vaguely mentioned as mere outlines.
However, in the plan of the new Berlin that was made public, it is possible to make out an east-west axis and a north-south axis.
The latter was planned to go from the new North station to a new South station which would have replaced the S-Bahn Papestraße station near a new town (Südstadt), which would be home to hundreds of thousands of inhabitants.
The western part of the east-west axis – including several new buildings – was finished in time to celebrate Hitler's 50th birthday in 1939: it ran from the Brandenburg gate to Adolf Hitler square (today named Theodor-Heuss-Platz) going through the new Großer Stern roundabout to which the Victory Column had been moved.
The preparatory work for the construction of the Great Dome and the Triumphal Arch, as well as for the entire north-south axis, included the demolition of the districts of Alsenviertel and Tiergarten, and the erection of the 'heavy loads structure' of the German Society for Soil Mechanics (DeGeBo) to study the resistance of soils composed of non-stratified materials (see page 110).
It also included the construction of railway tracks on a level with Priesterstraße and three tunnel segments for the road traffic where the two axes were planned to cross over. On the north-south axis Grazer Damm and the Tourist Office were created on the Place Ronde.
The new airport of Tempelhof is not specifically referred to in the project as plans for it had already been drawn up. It was practically finished when the war broke out and it would have been the central airport for the restructured capital of the Reich. Inaugurated for the 1936 Olympic Games, the stadium of the Reich, with all its annexes, would have been the heart Germania's sports installations. The embassies that were moved outside the district of Alsenviertel were supposed to form Germania's new district of embassies.
The head offices of Krupp in the capital of the Reich and those of many other companies in addition to the State's administrative buildings (for example, on Fehrbelliner Platz) were finished. The barracks and buildings of the army's General Staff

and the Reich's youth organisations were also built. The exceptional new buildings referred to in the plans and which were completely or almost completely finished, included the construction of the Faculty of the Technology of Armaments of the future university city; the Ministry of Popular Education and Propaganda; Goering's Ministry of Aviation; the enlarged Reichsbank; the Mint of the Reich and Molkenmarkt, the new administrative district with the new Mühlendamm lock. The new Mühlendamm bridge was not completed.

A sample section of the fourth motorway bypass around Berlin was tarmacked in front of the Telefunkenwerk factory of Zehlendorf (which brought together 37 of Berlin's old Telefunken workshops, see page 230).

On the edge of Spandau, a community of forced labourers, put there to build the Great Dome, was also created. After the declaration of war, only a few building sites commenced work. Speer, the Inspector General of Construction, put a stop to the demolition of old buildings for the north-south axis.

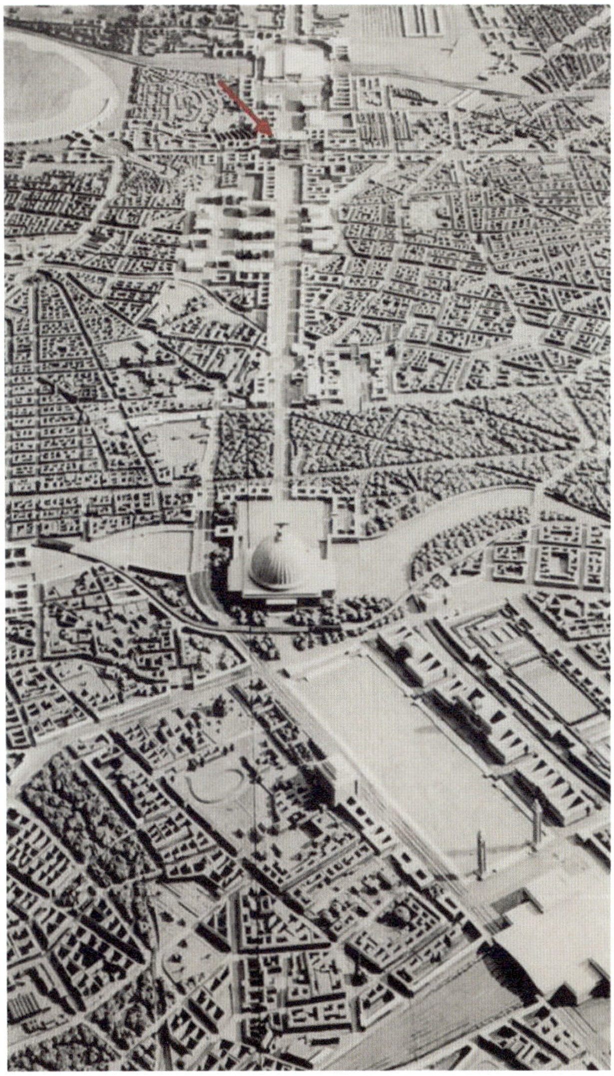

06.

Werner-Voß-Damm 54A
S1, 2, 41, 42 (Berlin Südkreuz)

THE PRISON OF DE LA GENERAL-PAPE-STRAßE

The very first concentration camp in the heart of Berlin

It is commonly agreed that any place where deported people, prisoners of war, political prisoners, or individuals considered as enemies of the state are kept under surveillance by the police or the army is a concentration camp.

Bearing this definition in mind, the prison of General Pope Street (Gefängnis Papestraße), set up in mid-March 1933 at number 54a Werner-Voß-Damm (an outbuilding of the complex whose entrance used to be on the General-Pape-Straße), is considered today as having been Nazi Germany's very first concentration camp.

Since March 2013, (exactly 80 years after it was built), the old cells in the cellar have become a memorial, with archives and an exhibition giving details of the terrible events which took place there at the beginning of the Third Reich.

Since some prisoners had been allocated a number or registration date, research work to identify the prison's victims became possible and helped piece together a certain number of facts.

The first known prisoner was recorded on 15-16 March 1933 and was allocated the number 43. The last identified prisoner to date bore the number 1842, dated November 1933. It would seem, therefore, that in the basement of this former barracks attached to the railway division (*Eisenbahntruppen*) of the Prussian army, about 2,000 people were kept prisoner there during 1933. They were mainly communists and socialists from the KPD (The German Communist Party), the SDP (The German Socialist Party), trade unionists and prominent Jews. At least 30 of them were beaten and tortured to death. To date, about 500 prisoners have been identified.

There were other concetration camps in Berlin (see next pages).

© Harry Weber

© Harry Weber

THE OTHER CONCENTRATION CAMPS IN BERLIN

Some may find it surprising that concentration camps existed in the very heart of the German capital, only days after the elections of 5 March 1933 which enabled the Nazi Party to seize power. It is important to remember, however, that Hitler had been appointed chancellor as early as 30 January 1933, and a month later, on the very day after the Reichstag fire on 27-28 February 1933, he had already declared a state of emergency against the communist threat.

Freedom of expression, the right to gather and the majority of civic rights were suspended, and the hunt for communists and Jews was unleashed. In 1933 alone, the regime took an estimated 200,000 political prisoners.

The German prisons soon began to overflow, and it is likely that the first makeshift concentration camps were built, even before the elections at the beginning of March. This is how inter-war Berlin, which had been a bastion of communism and German socialism and had 170,000 Jewish residents, became rife with places of imprisonment and torture. According to current research, there were no fewer than 220 such places, of which 11 could be considered as having been organised concentration camps, generally in the city centre, visible to all, and aimed at terrorising the population and discouraging anyone who was thinking of resisting.

In addition to the Papestraße prison, two others were built in March 1933 and were amongst some of the first camps in Berlin. One was in the machine room of the Prenzlauer Berg water tower, a building measuring 100 square metres, dynamited in 1935, where a number of political prisoners and enemies of the regime were held and tortured between March and June 1933. A commemorative plaque and a sign placed in front of the water tower located at number 23 Knaackstraße commemorate the victims (see page 176).

And another which was, by far, the capital's largest concentration camp was set up in the Columbiadamm former military prison in Kreuzberg, which stood on the south side of the avenue, on the corner of Golßener Straße.

© Harry Weber

Der Gefangene ...., Erich ......geb.d. ....

eingeliefert d. ....1......1933 .... Uhr hat die

Gefangenennummer ....235.....

Berlin,d. ....1. 4. ....

Kommando der Feldpoliz[ei]
Vernehmungsstelle

07.

Bessemerstraße 2–14
U6 (Alt-Tempelhof)
S2, 25, 26 (Priesterweg)
S41, 42, 45, 46 (Tempelhof)

VISIT TO THE MALZFABRIK

Strange chimneys not for evacuating air but for sucking it in

Although the Malzfabrik in Schöneberg is not an unfamiliar sight to Berliners, very few have been inside and know what these intriguing chimneys were used for.

One large structure topped with four distinctive metallic extensions towers over other tall brick structures in the site on Bessemerstraße. These *Darrhauben*, each weighing 3.3 tonnes, are commonly known as 'knights' (*Ritter* in German – which is cognate with *Reiter*, i.e. knight) as they seem to be straddling the roof.

These surprising features, which spin around separately, reacting to the slightest gust of wind, are not chimney caps: they were in fact designed to suck in the air and to carry it to the very heart of the building, where a constant stream of air was necessary for the production process.

The maltings belonged to the famous Schultheiss brewery, the main premises of which were located in Prenzlauer Berg (and which today is home to the Kulturbrauerei), but those premises in Pankow and Schöneberg were used exclusively for the production of malt.

During the guided tour of the partially conserved installations inside the Schöneberg site, visitors are taken on the *Malzreise* (the malt journey) showing the journey that the cereals (barley and wheat, for example) took before they were transformed into malt for the breweries in those days. It is a good way of getting to grips with brewer's jargon.

In the old *Tennenmälzerei* where the germination took place on a threshing floor, the grains were spread over a stone surface, sprayed with water and turned over with a fork or a rake by malters to air them. In the next phase in the Darren (drying kilns – the term comes from *dörren* – to dry/dehydrate), they were firstly aired to expel the water contained in the air coming from the 'knights' before being dried with hot air (basic drying) then very hot air ('the blast').

At a later date, 'pneumatic' malting was introduced: it was done in rectangular boxes with mechanical ventilation, then in rotating drums in which the grains could also be dried. These drums can be seen in the malthouse.

The pungent smell in the air and the sheer size of the place takes the visitor back in time to the atmosphere that must have once reigned there.

08.

Prellerweg 47–49
No bikes allowed
S2, 25, 26 (Priesterweg)

NATUR-PARK-SÜDGELÄNDE

A spectacular and unusual park

Inaugurated in 1999, Natur-Park Südgelände remains a mystery to many Berliners, thanks in part to its three rather inconspicuous entrances. The main entrance, located to the south, is the easiest to find and can be reached via the tunnel of Priesterweg S-Bahn station.
The public park was built on the grounds of a former marshalling yard that housed repair and maintenance workshops. It is now an amazing 18 hectare-long nature reserve – a stunning environment where nature has regained its rights after years of neglect, and where hundreds of plant and animal species (60 of which are endangered) appear to be flourishing. Dotted here and there are strange artistic installations and interesting relics from the past, such as an impressive 50 metre-high water tower once used to fill the tanks of steam locomotives, a huge turntable that allowed the locomotives to change direction (see page 158), and a spectacular locomotive from the 1940s.
During the golden era of the railroad, the entire Prussian railway network was organised around the capital in a star shape. Berlin served as the transfer point between all the lines, and transit between various stations at the gates of the city was operated by means of the Ringbahn. However, freight trains sometimes included wagons that travelled through the capital before going on to different destinations. This heralded the invention of marshalling yards, where trains were reassembled according to the destination of the wagons.
North of Prellerweg, Tempelhof Station was created in 1889 right where the Anhalt and Dresden lines merged. It was expanded several times, and over the years it became one of Berlin's most important marshalling yards. After the Second World War and the construction of the Berlin Wall, the station gradually fell out of use. In the early 1980s, plans to redevelop the site were about to materialise, but nature had taken over the site to such an extent that a popular initiative easily demonstrated that dozens of endangered species had found refuge there, so the area was protected.
Today, hikers travel along a path made up of grids attached to metal pipes, which are themselves installed on the old rails. This is to allow the flora to grow unhampered, the fauna to move freely around the site, and the rainwater to flow naturally.

50 3707-2

09.

Ceciliengärten 1–53
S1 (Friedenau)

ENTRANCE GATES OF THE CECILIENGÄRTEN

An aesthetic celebration of work

The Ceciliengärten district is a remarkable, little-known ensemble consisting of a pretty square, two beautiful statues (see opposite), beautiful entrance gates and interesting bas-reliefs on the theme of family and work.

Built by Heinrich Lassen between 1923 and 1927, and listed since 1995, the Ceciliengärten complex is first and foremost a social project.

Some of the medallions depict people farming the land or children playing, but most show various means of transport. They remind us that part of the complex was specifically made for the families of employees of the Berlin Public Transport Authority (BVG).

The complex is organised around the gardens (listed since 1977), which comprise an oblong public park surrounded by a promenade lined with chestnut trees. At the northern end is a large pool and at the southern end a pretty fountain topped by a fox.

Great care has been taken to highlight the two female statues by Georg Kolbe, which, although a good distance apart, face each other in the centre of the square. The arms of the first figure reach towards the sky; this is morning, stretching out her limbs after a good night's sleep. In contrast, the arms of the second one hang heavily; she represents the weariness of the evening and tiredness after a day's work.

Once again, these works highlight the purpose of these gardens: to celebrate the value of work from an aesthetic and architectural point of view.

AN ARTIST'S STUDIO IN A TOWER

The tower overlooking the gate on the south side is crowned by an octagonal pavilion made of oxidised copper in the Secession style. A commemorative plaque to the left of the archway indicates that this workshop was designed to accommodate artists, including the painter Hans Baluschek, a socialist artist who was revered during the Weimar Republic and who lived here on an honorary basis from 1929 to 1933.

COPIES OF GEORG KOLBE'S SCULPTURES IN BARCELONA

A copy of the sculpture entitled 'Morning' by Georg Kolbe, one of the pioneers of modern architecture, can be found in the courtyard of Mies van der Rohe's famous Barcelona Pavilion (1929) in the Spanish city.

39 38

10.

Traegerstraße 5
S41, 42 / U4 (Innsbrucker Platz)

EISACK TUNNEL

Why is the U4 line so short?

On the map of the Berlin metro network, the U4 line, shown in light yellow, catches the eye as it seems odd that it is so short: it runs for fewer than 3 kilometers through the Schöneberg neighbourhood from Innsbrucker Platz to Nollendorfplatz not far from the KaDeWe.
Inaugurated in 1910, before greater Berlin was founded in 1920, it was designed and constructed by the commune of Schöneberg (which was very wealthy at the time) strictly for the needs of the local population, which would explain why it only has five stations.
It was the first communal underground line in Germany and was run independently with no connecting lines to other stations, and therefore had its very own staff of mechanics and maintenance workshop.
Located on the site of what is now the Waldenburg-Oberschule, the workshop became redundant in 1926 when the U4 became part of the Berlin network. It closed several years later in 1932. Until this date, the trains of the U4 line were taken for repairs and maintenance through a tunnel of about 400 metres long starting from Innsbrucker Platz.
Today the group Tunnel Tours organises guided visits of this now-deserted tunnel which takes fans of Berlin 100 years back in time to tell the story of the U4 project and the technical achievement that it represented.
The tour, which lasts about two hours, starts on the platform of Innsbrucker Platz station before it leads down to the tunnel itself, a few minutes' walk away, thanks to a ladder which goes some ten metres down into the ground. Lamps are provided.

The Berlin underground network, comprising 26 lines and 475 km of metro and S-Bahn tracks, is one of the largest in the world after Seoul (940 km) and Beijing (690 km).

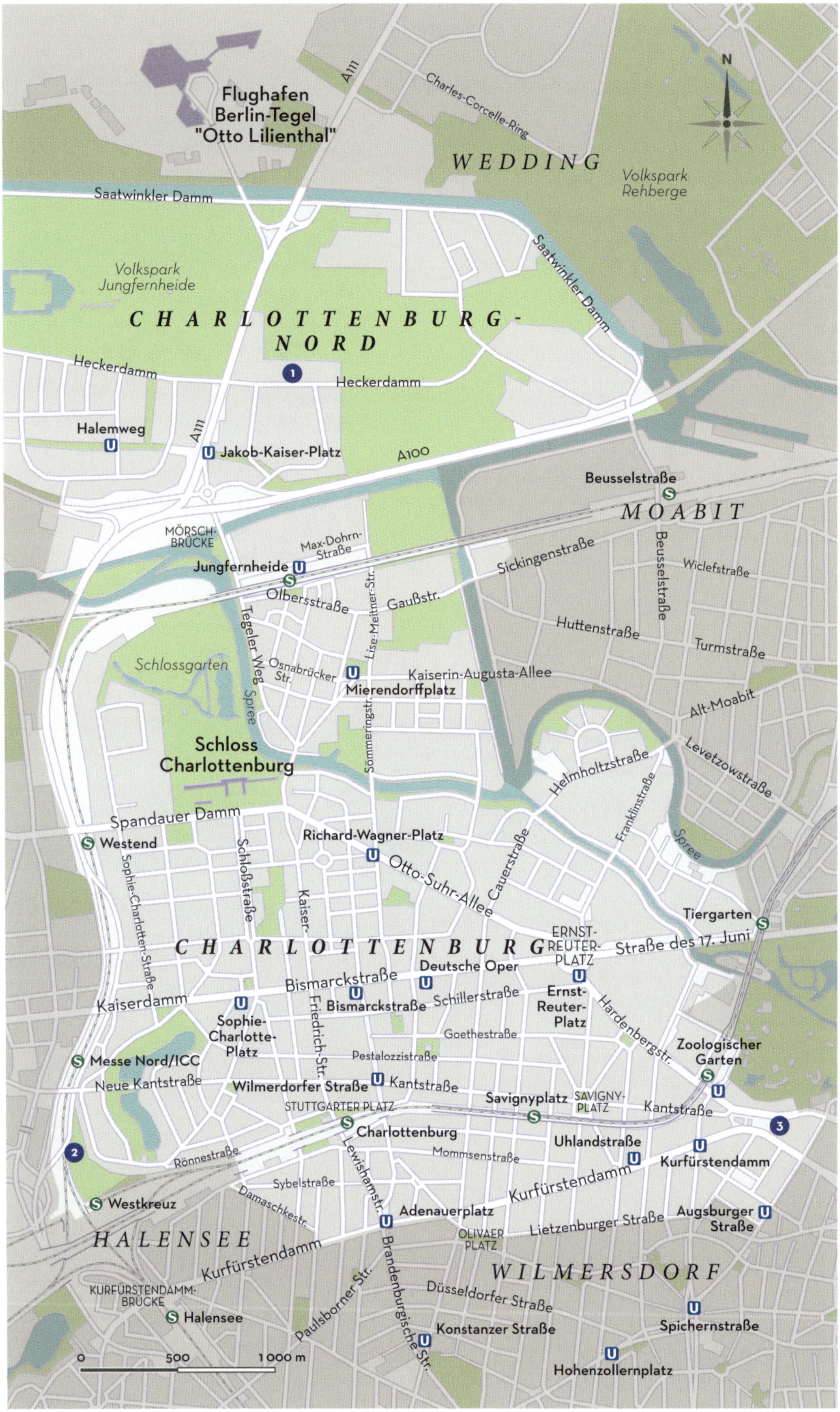
Flughafen Berlin-Tegel "Otto Lilienthal"
A111
Charles-Corcelle-Ring
WEDDING
N
Volkspark Rehberge
Saatwinkler Damm
Volkspark Jungfernheide
CHARLOTTENBURG-NORD
Heckerdamm
Halemweg
Jakob-Kaiser-Platz
A100
Beusselstraße
MOABIT
MÖRSCH-BRÜCKE
Max-Dohrn-Straße
Jungfernheide
Sickingenstraße
Wiclefstraße
Olbersstraße
Gaußstr.
Lise-Meitner-Str.
Huttenstraße
Turmstraße
Schlossgarten
Tegeler Weg
Osnabrücker Str.
Mierendorffplatz
Kaiserin-Augusta-Allee
Spree
Sömmeringstr.
Alt-Moabit
Schloss Charlottenburg
Helmholtzstraße
Levetzowstraße
Franklinstraße
Spandauer Damm
Westend
Richard-Wagner-Platz
Schloßstraße
Otto-Suhr-Allee
Cauerstraße
Sophie-Charlotten-Straße
Kaiser-Friedrich-Str.
Tiergarten
CHARLOTTENBURG
ERNST-REUTER-PLATZ
Straße des 17. Juni
Deutsche Oper
Bismarckstraße
Kaiserdamm
Schillerstraße
Ernst-Reuter-Platz
Hardenbergstr.
Sophie-Charlotte-Platz
Goethestraße
Zoologischer Garten
Messe Nord/ICC
Pestalozzistraße
Neue Kantstraße
Wilmerdorfer Straße
Kantstraße
Savignyplatz
SAVIGNY-PLATZ
STUTTGARTER PLATZ
Charlottenburg
Uhlandstraße
Mommsenstraße
Kurfürstendamm
Rönnestraße
Sybelstraße
Lewishamstr.
Westkreuz
Damaschkestr.
Adenauerplatz
Lietzenburger Straße
Augsburger Straße
HALENSEE
OLIVAER PLATZ
WILMERSDORF
Brandenburgische Str.
Paulsborner Str.
KURFÜRSTENDAMM-BRÜCKE
Halensee
Düsseldorfer Straße
Konstanzer Straße
Spichernstraße
Hohenzollernplatz
0
500
1 000 m
1
2
3

CHARLOTTENBURG

01.

Gedenkkirche der ev. Gemeinde
Heckerdamm 226
U7 (Jakob-Kaiser-Platz)

ALFRED HRDLICKA'S 'DANSE MACABRE'

A murderous dance

The 'Plötzenseer Totentanz' of the Protestant church, Gedenkkirche, in the north of Charlottenburg, is the work of Alfred Hrdlicka (1928–2009). From 1965 to 1972, he drew with lead pencils, charcoal, chalk and sanguine on 16 wooden panels measuring 3.5 metres high by just 1 metre in width. It is easy to recognise the barracks of the Plötzensee prison, still standing, where the Nazis executed almost 2,900 people, some of whom had not even been sentenced. In one night, known as the 'Bloody night of Plötzensee', under a constant stream of Allied bombs, 186 prisoners were hanged on butcher's hooks. Among them was the famous pianist Karl Robert Kreiten, who had been reported for making a joke against Hitler.

Even if the murders committed by the Nazis are not the unique subject of the panels, the walls of the shooting squad are depicted in the background with their arched windows and butcher's hooks. The artist adopts here the theme of the *danses macabres* of the Middle Ages, the artistic representations which, since the 15th century, had invoked death, for the most part taking the form of a skeleton who led the characters into their last dance. Hrdlicka uses this here to illustrate the violent deaths of the 20th century, representing, in addition to the bestial crimes of the Nazis, the death of a protester (Benno Ohnesorg) or that of a boxer in the ring (Sonny Banks). In the process, the artist shakes up traditional representations: a recurrent motif in the danse macabre, the death of a young girl, taking the form of a dance of death with a prostitute, in which the latter takes the initiative by attempting to seduce the skeleton.

The layout of the pews in the church is also unusual: they are arranged around the altar, which is in the centre.

A 10-minute walk away, the former execution hall of Plötzensee is open to the public: gedenkstaette-ploetzensee.de

02.

Halenseestraße 40
S3, 5, 7, 9, 41, 42, 46 (Westkreuz)

MONUMENT TO THE GLORY OF MOTORCYCLE RACERS

A rare Futurist monument that survived the Nazis

The only one of its kind in the world, this small monument stands alone on a traffic island, depicting two motorcycle racers in racing position on their motorcycles. It was placed where the steep, old northern bend of the AVUS racing circuit used to be, and represents the racers Ernst Henne on a BMW and Ewald Kluge on a DKW.

Heiner Fleischmann on his NSU is missing from the monument, even though he was drawn on the original plans.

Designed in 1938/39 by Max Esser (1885-1943), the sculpture, which could not be exhibited because of the war, is of real artistic interest: it is Berlin's only surviving Futurist sculpted group.

The Futurist movement was in fact one of the modernist artistic currents banned by the Nazis.

The monument escaped the systematic vetoes of the official Aryan art diktats thanks only to the enthusiasm of the Germans for racing in the 1930s.

Two of the three original sculptures, having survived in Noack's foundry workshop, were placed here in 1989.

The sculpture was mounted on a section of the original track surface of the famous sloping bend of the AVUS.

The granite column standing just next to the sculpture comes from the building at the entrance to the circuit.

There was a golden age for the AVUS motorcycle races (Automobil-Verkehrs-und Übungsstraße, literally 'automobile training and driving street') between 1922 and 1939, even if they were later outshone by motor car racing. On 19 September 1929, Ernst Jakob Henne (1904-2005), the first of two motorcycle star racers immortalised by Esser, riding his BMW WR 750, became the fastest man in the world on two wheels, covering a mile at 216.75 km/h. Between 1929 and 1937, no fewer than seven world speed records were broken thanks to him, the last one on 28 November 1937 with 279.5 km/h on a BMW 500. This record, which was held for almost 14 years, was broken by Wilhelm Herz in April 1951. Henne retired after his last record. With the war over, new races could take place from 1951 on the AVUS circuit. The motorcycling era came to an end for AVUS in 1966 (as did the motor car racing era in 1999).

03.

Budapester Straße 45
U1, 2, 3 (Wittenbergplatz)

BINNINGER'S CLOCK

A clock of sets? Not at all, they are nothing more than additions

With its soft curves and bright colours, the astonishing clock on the corner of the Europa-Center, next to the zoo, is not some forgotten pop art icon or an instrument used for communicating with extra-terrestrials from the film 'Close Encounters of the Third Kind'.
Clearly dating back to the 1970s, in keeping with the fashion that was then known in Germany as the *softline* design, this clock (for it is indeed a clock) with its round lamp on the top which goes on and off every second, is intriguing in itself – not to mention the various rows of lights that lead up to it.
In order to tell the time with it, the lights must be added up in the following way: at the very top, in the first row, each zone of lights represents five hours that have gone by, whereas each zone in the second row counts for one hour. On the third row, the 11 bars each represent five minutes, and in turn, each rectangle in the last row at the bottom is worth a minute. Therefore, if, as in the photo, 2 / 3 // 8 / 3 zones are lit up, then the clock indicates 13 hours (2 x 5 + 3) and 43 minutes (8 x 5 + 3). The seconds flash at the top but are not recorded. If we are to believe the explanations provided, the clock runs according to the mathematical theory of sets. But the system hiding behind these calculations has, in reality, very little to do with this famous theory, which imagines a construction of all the mathematical tools (numbers, functions, relations, etc) founded on a primitive notion of belonging to a set. It is extremely tempting to link it to this as, on the first and third rows, the hours and minutes are grouped together (and form therefore, mathematically speaking, sets), but this reasoning all, very quickly, comes to a dead end: the only concept at work being additions, as this mysterious clock turns out to be really nothing more than a sort of abacus.
Initially, this installation was a publicity stunt by Dieter Binninger, a clockmaker in Eppertshausen in Hesse. It was aimed at attracting attention to and advertising a rather ordinary wristwatch that he was working on. Binninger gave his 'Clock of Berlin' as a gift to Charlottenburg in1975. It remained in front of the Europa-Center opposite the church in memory of Kaiser-Wilhelm until 1995. As for Binninger's wristwatch, it was never put on the market, the development costs of the microprocessor were too high for him. On the other hand, a 'tabletop' version of the clock was put on the market and is still on sale today. In the days of incandescent lamps, the great Clock of Berlin was an 'electricity-guzzling' monster which cost a fortune. Every year, due to the vibrations caused by the traffic, the lightbulbs had to be changed by means of a hoisting platform, a system that was obviously not very cheap for Binninger. When he lost his life in a plane crash in 1991, the City of Berlin took over the maintenance until 1995. The clock was then dismantled to make savings, before being put back in 1996 thanks to entrepreneurs who continue to sponsor it today.

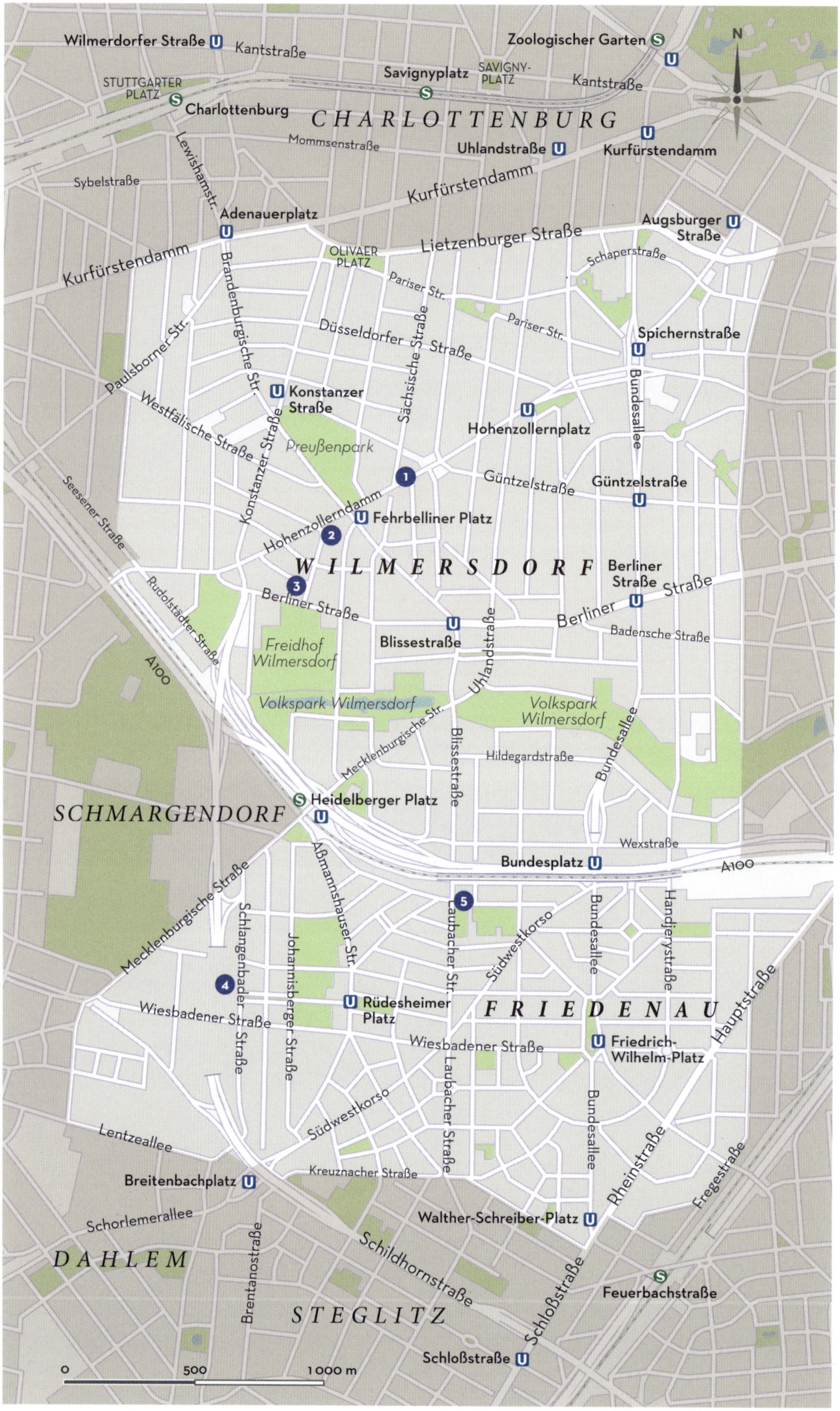
Wilmerdorfer Straße
Kantstraße
Zoologischer Garten
Savignyplatz
SAVIGNY-PLATZ
Kantstraße
STUTTGARTER PLATZ
Charlottenburg
CHARLOTTENBURG
Mommsenstraße
Uhlandstraße
Kurfürstendamm
Sybelstraße
Lewishamstr.
Kurfürstendamm
Adenauerplatz
Augsburger Straße
Lietzenburger Straße
OLIVAER PLATZ
Schaperstraße
Kurfürstendamm
Pariser Str.
Pariser Str.
Brandenburgische Str.
Paulsborner Str.
Düsseldorfer Straße
Sächsische Straße
Spichernstraße
Konstanzer Straße
Bundesallee
Westfälische Straße
Hohenzollernplatz
Preußenpark
Konstanzer Straße
Seesener Straße
Güntzelstraße
Güntzelstraße
Hohenzollerndamm
Fehrbelliner Platz
WILMERSDORF
Berliner Straße
Rudolstädter Straße
Berliner Straße
Berliner Straße
Uhlandstraße
Badensche Straße
Friedhof Wilmersdorf
Blissestraße
A100
Volkspark Wilmersdorf
Volkspark Wilmersdorf
Mecklenburgische Str.
Blissestraße
Hildegardstraße
Bundesallee
Heidelberger Platz
SCHMARGENDORF
Wexstraße
Bundesplatz
A100
Aßmannshauser Str.
Mecklenburgische Straße
Schlangenbader Straße
Johannisberger Straße
Laubacher Str.
Südwestkorso
Bundesallee
Handjerystraße
Rüdesheimer Platz
FRIEDENAU
Hauptstraße
Wiesbadener Straße
Wiesbadener Straße
Friedrich-Wilhelm-Platz
Südwestkorso
Laubacher Straße
Bundesallee
Lentzeallee
Rheinstraße
Breitenbachplatz
Kreuznacher Straße
Fregestraße
Schorlemerallee
Walther-Schreiber-Platz
DAHLEM
Brentanostraße
Schildhornstraße
Schloßstraße
Feuerbachstraße
STEGLITZ
Schloßstraße
0
500
1000 m
N
1
2
3
4
5

WILMERSDORF – FRIEDENAU

01.

Nassauische Straße 66–67
U2, 3 (Hohenzollernplatz)

THE STAINED-GLASS WINDOWS OF THE CHURCH ON HOHENZOLLERNPLATZ

Exceptional plays of light

Built between 1930 and 1933 by architect Ossip Klarwein, the Kirche am Hohenzollernplatz (Church on Hohenzollernplatz) is hardly a hidden gem, with its 66-meter-tall steeple, 40-meter-long nave, and 20-meter-high interior. But who, apart from the parishioners, has visited its exceptional interior?

Upon entering the church, one is indeed struck by the exceptional play of light created by the side stained-glass windows and the immense stained-glass window behind the altar: these cast shades of yellow, red, and blue throughout the vast church, inviting visitors and parishioners alike to sit for a moment and enjoy the spectacle.

This feature did not exist when the building was first constructed: the church was in fact largely destroyed on November 22, 1943, during an Allied bombing raid; the original organ, frescoes, and paintings were almost entirely destroyed in the ensuing fire. The current beautiful stained-glass windows are recent: they were created in 1990–91 by the German artist Achim Freyer.

Every Saturday at noon, during NoonSong, a Mass is sung by a professional choir.

The church is a fine example of Backsteinexpressionismus (Brick Expressionism), an architectural style typical of northern Germany.

02.

Fehrbelliner Platz 4
U2, 3, 7 (Fehrbelliner Platz)

THE RED LETTERBOX OF THE FEHRBELLINER PLATZ

A discrete souvenir of British occupation

On the front of number 4 Fehrbelliner Platz, a former Nazi building which was home to the general management of the DAF, the Deutsche Arbeitsfront (German Labour Front), a discrete, red letterbox with inscriptions written in English, goes relatively unnoticed ...

The typically English-style telephone box standing proudly nearby, reminds us that the building, which was not damaged in the bombings during the war, was converted into the headquarters of the British occupying forces in 1945.

Named Lancaster House, the building shared the same name as the legendary British Bombardier plane called Avro Lancaster, which was used during World War II. In 1954, the British Army Headquarters moved to the former Sportforum, on the site of the 1936 Olympics. But the British had good memories of the premises on Fehrbelliner Platz, which was full of charm. The subjects of Her Majesty had a reputation. They liked keeping to themselves, for example, at the British officers' mess club located on Thüringer Allee, in the very place where the Berlin's ice skating club had been based before the war broke out. It was the Queen's visits in 1965, 1978 and 1987, that made the British more appealing to Berliners. In May 1987, the year of the city's 750th anniversary, Queen Elizabeth stayed in Berlin for two days with her husband, Prince Philip. She made a speech at the Palace of Charlottenburg, addressing Berlin in German, and had tea at Bellevue Palace with German Federal president Richard von Weizsäcker. She then celebrated her own birthday (the celebrations of which are traditionally held in May instead of April because of the weather) on the Maifeld, which belonged to the Olympic site and which was being used by British troops.

On 5 March 1987, Her Majesty's ambassador, Sir Julian Leonard Bullar, and the British occupation sector's commander in Berlin, Patrick Guy Brooking, had already given the telephone booth and the red letterbox to the Germans. It was an official gift from the British occupying power. In comparison, the Americans had donated an entire library: the Amerika-Gedenkbibliothek.

4
POST OFFICE
NEXT COLLECTION

03.

Brienner Straße 7–8
U2, 3, 7 (Fehrbelliner Platz)

THE LAHORE AHMADIYYA MOVEMENT MOSQUE

A jewel of Indo-Islamic architecture

The magnificent Wilmersdorf Mosque (also known historically as the *Berliner Moschee* or *Ahmadiyya-Moschee*) is the oldest mosque in Germany. Built between 1924 and 1928 for the Ahmadiyya Anjuman Isha'at Islam (AAIIL – Lahore Ahmadiyya Movement for the Propagation of Islam), it consists of two 32 metre-high minarets detached from the main building, and a dome 26 metres high and 10 metres in diameter. The prayer hall can accommodate about 400 worshippers.

Designed by Berlin architect K.A. Hermann, the mosque is reminiscent of the Mughal architecture of the Taj Mahal.

Current owner and builder AAIIL financed its construction solely through donations.

As has always been the case, the mosque is 'open for worship to Muslims of all Mohammedan nations and all religious currents without distinction.' Simply put, it is open to all, every day.

During the Nazi period, the Berlin branch of the AAIIL and its mosque played an important role in helping Jews flee Germany.

However, the Nazis had used the mosque for propaganda purposes. For example, the SS received Mohammed Amin al-Husseini – the Grand Mufti of Jerusalem and a known anti-Semite – as a guest of honour.

04.

Schlangenbader Straße 18
U3 (Rüdesheimer Platz)

A104 MOTORWAY TUNNEL BUILDING

A motorway running through a building

In the district of Wilmersdorf, the *Schlange* (snake) in the street name Schlangenbader Straße refers to the largest housing estate in Europe. At 600 metres long, with a maximum height of 45 metres, it accommodates 3,500 tenants across 1,215 apartments. Including accessory constructions, there are actually 1,700 accommodations.

But its most unique feature becomes apparent when seen from above; the entire building straddles a stretch of motorway, the A104 (Abzweig Steglitz), which connects the A100 motorway with Hohenzollerndamm in the north and the B1 (via Schildhornstraße) in the south.

At the point where Wiesbadener Straße intersects the building, roughly in the middle, the motorway tunnel can be seen embedded in a concrete box, connecting the two halves of the residential complex like a bridge. To protect the accommodations from vibrations, the motorway box does not touch the walls of the superstructure; it rests on rubber pads, which in turn rest on enormous pillars anchored in the ground.

In corridors or stairwells, such as on Wiesbadener Straße, a faint 'knock-knock-knock' can be heard – the only reminder that there is constant traffic beneath. This is what the locals call the heartbeat of the complex. There are some 54,000 beats a day; that's the average number of vehicles passing through.

According to residents, nothing can be heard in the apartments, even on the fourth floor just above the roads.

Completed in 1980, the Berlin Snake embodies the fever that gripped the West at the time, and particularly its infatuation with rooftop constructions, which almost without exception remained at the planning stage. Oswald Mathias Ungers (OMU), a well-known name in Western architecture, had proposed the construction of a 20-storey superstructure straddling the 500 kilometre-long motorway between Hamburg and Frankfurt am Main.

Berlin was fortunate (or perhaps unfortunate) that money from Western subsidies flowed in during the time Germany was divided, so it was able to build not only a city motorway (which is still in the process of being built), but also the snake.

degewo

05.

Niedstraße 4
U3 (Rüdesheimer Platz)

HOUSE AT NIEDSTRAßE 4

An incredible façade

The *Drachenhaus* (dragon house) at Niedstraße 4 is a spectacular building dating back to 1899. Its façade is decorated with a series of sculptures of characters apparently linked to the theme of enjoying life (note the vine, the beer mug, the monk and his belly) while being careful (the owl and his mirror) to avoid the harmful consequences (the dragon, the crow) of indulging too much. The sculptures, based on the drawings of an unknown artist, were produced by the Hermann Noak foundry, which was established two years earlier in Friedenau (now located in Charlottenburg), and to which Berlin owes the casting of many major works.

Supported by two gargoyle-shaped corbels, the oriel window is topped by a large winged dragon and shamrocks that appear under the windows of the second floor.

In the centre, a monk (with a rather prominent belly that demonstrates just what a *bon vivant* he is) emerges from a barrel marked with the year the building was inaugurated. Originally, he brandished a mug of beer in his outstretched left hand, but it has since disappeared.

Two branches of vines are tied together around him with a ribbon, from which hang a large key and a pair of shoes.

On either side of the monk, two large birds are perched between vine leaves. On the left is a raven holding a spoon in its beak, perhaps a reference to painter Adolph Menzel's 'Kinderalbum', a book of illustrations for children that features a raven stealing a silver spoon. On the right, an owl holds up a mirror, probably referring to the acrobat *Eulenspiegel*, which literally translates as 'the mirror of the owl'.

Above the monk's head, a faun appears to be curled around a large hourglass and pointing at it; it is depicted with two wings and a halo decorated with 17 ears of wheat, a rare variation on the faun theme.

Finally, directly beneath the gable windows, surrounded by wings as cherubs often are, is the head of a 10-year-old child with a knot in her hair; she is strangely reminiscent of the characteristic face (particularly recognisable by her prominent chin) of Alice in Wonderland as she was imagined by Sir John Tenniel.

Niedstraße is commonly called the 'Literaturmeile' ('Literary Mile') because of the many writers who lived here during the 20th century: the most famous were Erich Kästner (Niedstraße 5); Günter Grass (Niedstraße 13); and Uwe Johnson, who lived at Niedstraße 14, which is also where the legendary Kommune I was founded in 1967.

Kurt-Schumacher-Platz
Holländerstraße
Franz-Neumann-Platz
N
Residenzstraße
Markstraße
Afrikanische Straße
Müllerstr.
Dubliner Straße
Bristolstr.
Barfusstr.
Edinburger Straße
Schillerpark
Ungarnstraße
Osloer Straße
NACHTIGAL-PLATZ
Rehberge
Reinickendorfer Straße
WEDDING
Seestraße
Afrikanische Straße
Togostraße
Nauener Platz
Seestraße
LEOPOLD-PLATZ
Volkspark Rehberge
Transvaalstraße
Müllerstr.
Brüsseler Str.
Leopoldplatz
Seestraße
Amrumer Str.
Luxemburger Str.
Humboldthain
Saatwinkler Damm
Wedding
Föhrer Str.
Amrumer Straße
Reinickendorfer Straße
Lynarstraße
Chausseestraße
Friedrich-Krause-Ufer
LUDWIG-HOFFMANN-BRÜCKE
Westhafen
Boyenstr.
Beusselstraße
Quitzowstraße
Perleberger Straße
Heidestraße
Birkenstraße
Sickingenstraße
Beusselstraße
Wiclefstraße
Birkenstraße
Lehrter Straße
Scharnhorststraße
MOABIT
Stromstraße
Rathenower Straße
Fritz-Schloß-Park
Huttenstraße
Turmstraße
Turmstraße
Seydlitzstraße
MITTE
Turmstraße
Alt-Moabit
Alt-Moabit
Invalidenstraße
Hauptbahnhof
Berlin Hauptbahnhof
LESSING-BRÜCKE
Helmholtzstr.
Levetzowstraße
Paulstraße
Bellevue
Franklinstraße
Spree
Hansaplatz
Altonaer Str.
Brandenburger Tor
Straße des 17. Juni
Tiergarten
Straße des 17. Juni
Ernst-Reuter-Platz
Hofjägerallee
TIERGARTEN
Potsdamer Platz
Tiergartenstraße
Hardenbergstr.
Zoologischer Garten
Reichpietschufer
Budapester Straße
SAVIGNY-PLATZ
Kantstraße
Savignyplatz
LÜTZOW-PLATZ
Lützowstraße
Linkstraße
Kurfürstendamm
Kurfürstenstraße
Potsdamer Straße
Mendelssohn-Bartholdy-Park
Uhlandstraße
Augsburger Straße
Wittenbergplatz
Kurfürstenstraße
Gleisdreieck
Lietzenburger Str.
Nollendorfplatz
Kurfürstenstr.
WILMERSDORF
0
500
1000 m
1
2
3
4
5
6
7
8
9
10

WEDDING – MOABIT – TIERGARTEN

01.

Scharnweberstraße 158
U6 (Afrikanische Straße or Kurt-Schumacher-Platz)

THE WEDDING SAND DUNE

A very secret sand dune

On the SUZ (gardening school) site with its educational gardens, on the edge of the Rehberge park, there is an intriguing, secret sand dune that can be visited if booked in advance.

It was formed around the end of a glacial period called the Weichselian, or Vistulian, as it takes its name from the Vistulia river. When the last glaciers disappeared from this era around 12,000 years ago, they left behind large zones scattered with fallen rocks, moraines and sandbanks. The vegetation slowly began to take root, allowing the wind to blow the sand around freely, spreading much of it over the surrounding area and forming it into dunes.

Over the millennia, human intervention has caused vegetation to become denser with, for example, the planting of hedges to protect meadows and fields. In the 18th century, the systematic planting of dunes took place at the same time as the extraction of sand reduced the number of inland dunes.

Luckily, the plans for the Friedrich-Ebert-Siedlung workers' housing, which was supposed to be built here in 1929, were shelved. The Wedding dune therefore remained intact until it was partly integrated into the gardening school in 1950. In 1976, the area was registered as a protected natural site before a global conservation and development plan was drawn up at the end of the 1980s.

In 2002, the Wedding dune was given extra protection when the atypical vegetation of brambles and beeches was removed. Only the original types of dune vegetation, Scots pines and oaks, were left to flourish. The undying commitment of the German Federation for the Protection of Nature (NABU) in Berlin has gradually given the dune its initial appearance back. Invasive plants are now systematically removed, and the layer of humus, which is 40 cm thick in some places, is also regularly reduced.

The dune can be partially seen from the car park of the neighbouring DIY store, but for a closer look at the oldest mound of sand from the glacial period in Berlin-Mitte, volunteers can join the NABU group of Berlin-Mitte to help maintain the dune.

02.

Badstraße 38–39
U8 (Pankstraße)

THE SPA PAVILION BAS-RELIEF

A district named after the thermal baths

On the corner of Badstraße and Travemünder Straße, on the last floor of the west-facing side of the house, there is a discreet bas-relief of a pavilion with a roof in the shape of a pagoda bearing the Latin inscription '*In fonte salus*' ('health from the source').

This serves as a reminder that there was once a pavilion here which housed the old thermal fountain and gave its name to the surrounding neighbourhood. A walk through covered walkway number 39 will also take you to the old spa, which is now used as the local library. Although there are no particularly interesting remnants of its past to be seen inside, on the outside, the building's lovely frontages have been preserved.

This is where a mineral spring, possessing excellent medicinal properties according to studies carried out by the renowned Berlin chemist Andreas Sigismund Marggraf (1709–1782), was discovered in the middle of the 18th century. This chemist was also the inventor of beet sugar. King Frederick II was keen on thermal spa treatment (he went to take the waters in Pyrmont every year), and naturally gave his blessing to the project of a thermal spa in Berlin, having had the results of Marggraf's studies confirmed by the Obercollegium Medicum of Berlin.

This is how the court's apothecary, Heinrich Wilhelm Behm (1708–1780), obtained the right to build a thermal spa so that people could experience the remarkable benefits of this water by drinking it or bathing in it. Behm got to work quickly: the spring was enclosed with a pretty brick wall which was then covered by a beautiful pavilion, the copy of which on the library frontage is particularly realistic. Large gardens with spa buildings were created around the fountain. Amongst the visitors were people suffering mostly from rheumatism and eye disorders. In 1799, Luise, the young queen of Prussia, graced the spa with her presence. The baths were then renamed 'Luisenbad' in her honour.

The thermal spa continued to be popular until the middle of the 19th century.

In the large spa resorts, there were many visitors who wanted just to enjoy themselves, and so inns, dance halls and casinos sprang up around Badstraße – all of this came to a sudden end in 1888 when the construction of a drain ruined the spring that had once offered multiple health benefits. All attempts to restore it were in vain.

The baths of Badstraße (*bad* means 'bath') have given their name to the Gesundbrunnen (Fountain of health) district as well as to Brunnenstraße (Fountain Street).

IN FONTE SALUS
LUISENHAUS

03.

Thomasiusstraße 5
U9 (Turmstraße)

THE FAÇADE OF THOMASIUSSTRAßE 5

Jugendstil metaphysics

Number 5 Thomasiusstraße in Moabit has an extraordinary Jugendstil facade, created in 1902 by the architect Hans Landé and the sculptor Carl Caspary, with the enormous face of a bearded man, decorated with numerous elements cast in bronze.
With its open mouth, the face is undoubtedly that of God the creator, who created the world with his words.
Duality, represented by two fauns of opposite sexes on either side of the pediment, spouts from his mouth: they are the two contradictory fundamental principles of the one reality, the Yin and the Yang, the conflict between them being illustrated by the fact that the female faun is playing unbearable music to the male faun, who is covering his ears so that he cannot hear it.
Just below this, on a level with the windows of the top floor, the roles change: on the right, the man seems disconcerted by his wife's annoyance, portrayed on the left.
Two floors further down, this conflict is associated with the double struggle taking place between a bull (without horns?) and a snake, an image of the antagonism between masculine and feminine energies.
Between these two scenes of combat, the columns separating the windows are covered with sunflowers. As it constantly follows the sun's course, the sunflower has, since ancient times, represented the search for truth in love.
Here, the artist invites the onlooker to reflect on the nature of the divine which is at work in duality.
By placing a landscape representing Athens's Acropolis (on the left) and Cairo's Sphinx (on the right), above the main entrance, the architect suggests that the solution to the problem is to be found in the philosophy and wisdom of Ancient Egypt and Ancient Greece.

04.

Turmstraße 91
U9 (Turmstraße)

THE HALL OF THE MOABIT COURTHOUSE

A grand show

Courthouses are not often considered as places which can be visited but they are, in fact, by definition public places which are open to the general public. The Kriminalgericht (criminal court) of Moabit is no exception. Built at the beginning of the 20th century, it provides a truly great show for visitors.
Behind the security checks, the huge entrance hall looks like the nave of a Gothic cathedral.
Incredibly modern-looking Art Deco lights hang from its keystones. KCG, which stands for *Kaiserliches Criminalgericht* (Imperial Court-house), is written in stylised lettering on the terracotta floor tiles and serves as a reminder that this is a construction dating back to Wilhelmian times. The hall, which is surrounded by galleries, has three floors connected by the crisscrossing flights of a magnificent staircase, just like something out of an etching by Piranesi. Three vaulted gates are surmounted by baroque allegorical sculptures: above the righthand gate, lies and truth; to the left, quarrels (*Streitsucht*) and leniency (*Friedfertigkeit*); and finally, at the back, forgiveness and justice bearing the sword of judgement, which will decide between guilt and innocence.

ATTENDING A TRIAL

It is possible to attend ongoing trials. Other than being an interesting experience, the architectural quality of some courtrooms make them worth a visit. Ask at reception which rooms are being used for hearings on the day you visit.

THE LARGEST COURTHOUSE IN EUROPE

All the hearings concerning misdemeanours and crimes committed in Berlin are held here, up to 300 a day. The Kriminalgericht of Moabit is the largest courthouse in Europe with its 240 working judges, 80 court administrators and 300 prosecutors. It is twinned with the remand prison, the (*Untersuchungsgefängnis*) of Moabit (Alt-Moabit 12a), situated a few yards away where an average of 1,300 people are held, awaiting trial.

STUNNINGLY MODERN FOR ITS TIME

The building, inaugurated in 1906, was stunningly modern for its time. The courthouse was the first building in the capital to be entirely equipped with electricity, and was designed with its own electric power station, running water distribution network (including its own water tower), central heating, a telephone network and numerous lifts. Originally made up of 21 courtrooms, the building was repeatedly extended from the 1950s onwards, so much so that it is difficult today for visitors to find their way through the maze of corridors and staircases.

05.

Invalidenstraße 50–51
S3, 5, 7, 9, 75 / U55 (Hauptbahnhof)

AN OASIS OF GREENERY IN THE HAMBURGER BAHNHOF

A souvenir of the train station's turntable

Opposite the famous Hamburger Bahnhof Museum of Contemporary Art, in the buildings of the eponymous former train station, is a forecourt composed of a circular garden surrounding an oasis of greenery, all perfectly contained within a boxwood hedge. The hedge echoes the turntable that used to be there until the closure of the station in 1884, and which made it possible for locomotives to turn and travel back in the opposite direction.

When railroads first appeared at the end of the 1830s, in order to limit noise and pollution, trains were not permitted to run through cities. Hence a station known as a terminus (see page 66) was built beyond the city boundaries, close to various points of access. The Hamburg terminus was originally near *Neues Tor* (New Door), which opened onto the current Robert-Koch-Platz on the city side.

However, the concept of a terminus raised a number of technical problems, not least how to get locomotives to go back the opposite way after reaching their destination.

The issue was solved by installing turntables on which the locomotives would rotate to face the required direction – hence the need for a forecourt where a turntable, as well as enormous entrance archways (to allow locomotives to pass by before and after turning), could be installed.

The Hamburger Bahnhof perfectly illustrates this solution: after entering the station, the locomotive passed through the left archway, rotated on the platform – now indicated by the oasis of greenery – and exited in the opposite direction through the archway on the right.

As for the passengers, rather than use the central archway, they entered the station hall via more modest doors at the sides – following the subsequent construction of lateral wings, the doors are no longer visible.

It is possible to see two turntables in a near-original state at the Technik Museum. They correspond to the turntables of the Anhalter Bahnhof terminus.

06.

Opposite number 140 Alt-Moabit
S3, 5, 7, 9 / U55 (Hauptbahnhof)

THE STAIRS OF THE ULAP

Last minute barbarity

Opposite the recently inaugurated Federal Home Office in Moabit (2015), some very old, authentic stone steps have an unnatural slant to them. Skinny trees grow between the steps. In 1879, the first visitors climbed these stairs on their way to the land's exhibition centre (ULAP) which had just been inaugurated. The first exhibition was on industry, the second on hygiene, and others followed until the mid-1920s. In 1936, the year of the Olympic games, the centre hosted Berlin's German aeronautic collection with the largest plane in the world, a German, civil flying boat: the Dornier Do X.
But to save this area from the speculation of real estate promoters, it would take more than the sole distinction of this historic centre and its exhibitions. In 1927, the building work carried out for the Stadtbahn uncovered 126 corpses, revealing that the site had been used as a graveyard; it harboured a considerable number of victims of political assassinations from the beginning of the Weimar Republic, and was also the scene of the cold-blooded executions perpetrated by the SS at the very end of the war in 1945. They were the remains of Spartacists who had been taken out of the prison cells in Lehrter Straße, the barracks of Moabit and the cells of Kriminalgericht of Moabit to be executed on the site of the exhibition centre. In March 1933, in a room located under the restaurant of the exhibition pavilion, the SA tortured the lawyer Günther Joachim to death. The bloody history of this place came to a climax with the murder of 16 political prisoners from the prison of Moabit on the Lehrter Straße on the night of 23 April 1945. Most of them were accused of being part of the plot on 20 July 1944, an attempted assassination of Adolf Hitler. At the very last minute, the SS made the prisoners go down these stairs, pretending that it was for a transfer due to enemy advances. They were forced to line up, and the SS shot them from behind. The sole survivor was a young communist called Herbert Kosney, as the bullet that was fired into the nape of his neck missed his spine.
Thanks to the information that he provided, the Soviet military police found the bodies a few days later. What became known as the 'Sonnets of Moabit' were found in geographer Albrecht Haushofer's jacket pocket, and included the sonnet entitled 'Schuld' ('Guilt'): 'Early on I saw the whole tragedy coming – / I said it – but not loudly or clearly enough!'

07.

Alsenviertel, Spreebogen
Otto-von-Bismarck-Allee 4A
S3, 5, 7, 9 (Hauptbahnhof) / S1, 2, 25 (Brandenburger Tor)
U55 (Bundestag)

THE PAPER LEAVES OF THE SWISS EMBASSY

An unexpected work of art

On the way into the (covered) entrance of the remarkable Embassy of Switzerland, the ground is permanently littered with paper leaves. Do not take this for a lack of zeal on the part of the person in charge of cleaning the embassy: these (paper) leaves are part of an artist's work. Pipilotti Rist is the artist, as we learn from reading a small text on the right-hand wall. Once every twelve minutes, in the contemporary-style entrance hall designed in 2001 by the architects Diener&-Diener, a paper leaf flutters down from the ceiling. The machine (if you look up you can see the hole that the leaves fall through) was built in Switzerland by Dimitri Westermann (Smokeball).

The paper leaves represent different types of tree leaves (maple, oak, ginkgo, lime and vine). On each leaf there is a photo of the leaf on one side and, on the other side, a short message such as: *Du bist ein Sonnenaufgang* ('you are a sunrise').

Written, in theory, in one of the four official languages of Switzerland (only messages written in German could be seen when we were there and the twelve-minute intervals were not always respected), the poetic texts are not linked to each other. This flutter of leaves littering the floor is a popular attraction as it is not the kind of artwork that you would normally expect to find in such an institution.

The artist sees these leaves 'as a metaphor for democracy, they are the ambassadors of a universal message'. For this reason, visitors are encouraged to take them away with them.

Originally planned to last for ten years, the work of art has been kept on by the embassy. Visits to see the machine which sends the leaves fluttering down must be booked in advance.

08.

Straße des 17. Juni
U9 (Hansaplatz) / S3, 5, 7, 9 (Tiergarten (Berlin)

THE KERBS OF GERMANIA

Thankfully, there are limits

Often hidden by tourist buses, two kerbs appear to have mysteriously sunk into the asphalt sidewalk of the Straße des 17. Juni. They can be seen clearly opposite the Soviet memorial on the sidewalk running along Tiergarten Park.
What appear to be markings left from construction works actually correspond to the first metre of the north-south axis of Germania, Hitler and Speer's intended new capital (see page 112), of which the current Straße des 17. Juni was the first part. To the west, the east-west axis had already been completed in time for Hitler's 50th birthday, 20 April 1939.
After the Soviet victory over Nazi Germany, the Soviets knowingly chose this site to erect their memorial. Indeed, as it blocks the access to what was intended to be the world's largest building, the Great Hall (Große Halle), and where the current German Chancellery currently stands, the memorial symbolises the crushing of Hitler's plans for world dominance
The huge forecourt of the Great Hall was intended to run alongside Hitler's giant palace and the Reichstag, which would have appeared very small in comparison.

By measuring the distance between the two preserved kerbs on the first metre of the north-south axis, it is possible to establish that the axis would have been 120 metres wide.
At 75 metres wide, the east-west axis located right behind is already Germany's widest street. Given that no traffic lights were planned for Hitler's Via Triumphalis in the southern direction, one would need to have been super human to cross the street successfully.
In order to ensure traffic safety at the crossroads of these two axes, huge tunnels were planned.
The first sections of these tunnels were constructed and are now preserved. Their ventilation shafts are located in the park, at the next intersection to the west of Bremer Weg.

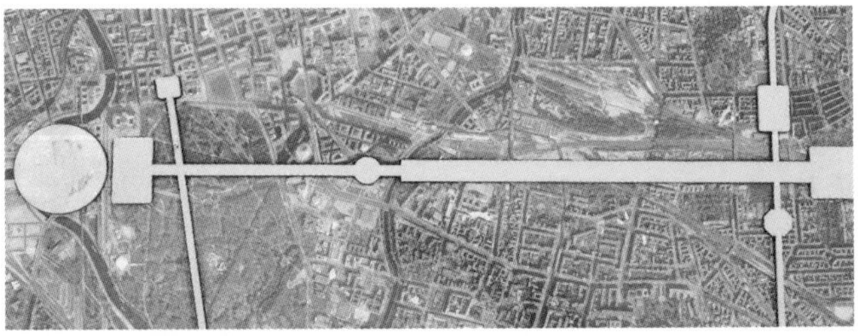

09.

Straße des 17. Juni
S3, 5, 7, 9 (Tiergarten) / U9 (Hansaplatz)

THE GAS STREET LAMPS OF THE OPEN AIR MUSEUM

The most romantic museum in Berlin

To get to the most romantic museum in Berlin, it is an easy ride from the S-Bahn Tiergarten station to the Zoo underground stop. The open air museum can be visited whilst walking through the park of the same name. It is free of charge and really worth seeing, especially at night when it is lit up, giving the visitor a feeling of being taken back in time.

The 'open air museum' has the largest historic collection in the world of gas street lamps. GASAG, the oldest local gas distribution company, has sponsored the museum since 1978, when this lovely idea became reality. To this day, Berlin has remained the capital of gas street lamps: in 2009, there were still 44,000 in working order, more than anywhere else in the world.

The story of these street lamps in Berlin began with the Prussian Home Secretary who appointed the Imperial Continental Gas Association (ICGA) of London to set up the gas street lighting in Berlin. The first gas works (the gas street lighting company) was built on the site of the open air swimming pool in Kreuzberg, and in September 1826 the first gas street lamps, powered by underground pipes, lit up Unter den Linden. By 1846, the ICGA had provided the town with a 100-km-long gas distribution network. After this date, the Berliners progressively took control of the production of gas for lighting, heating and cooking.

West Berlin continued to produce its own town gas until the 1980s, even if the rest of Western Germany used the natural gas supplied by the East. The town gas was actually produced in West Berlin, as was the electricity, from coal and petrol. Both had to be shipped by train from the West. With the easing of relations between the east and west, from 1983, West Berlin was also supplied by the Russian natural gas pipeline. However, the latter is partly converted into town gas and stored in large underground gas reserves ... Paranoia or mere precaution?

In Western Germany, gas street lighting rapidly disappeared in the 1970s and 80s. However, at the very same time these beautiful gas street lamps were to be given a new lease of life in the Tiergarten. To fight against vandalism, a poem by Erich Mühsam, an anarchist writer, was quoted on the public benches. It tells the story of a revolutionary who was a lamplighter by trade, and who protested when his companions tore down the street lamps to set up barricades. 'I'm a lamplighter of this good lighting. I beg you to leave it alone. If we cut off this source of lighting, no one will be able to see anything'.

10.

Versuchsanstalt Dynamik Maritimer Systeme
Müller-Breslau-Straße 15
S3, 5, 7, 9 (Tiergarten)

A VISIT TO THE UT2

The world's largest cavitation testing station

Viewing the 35-metre-high UT2 building from afar (a hybrid of giant pink pipelines and stranded container ships), it's hard to imagine the interior. But inside, it's like a cargo vessel dedicated to scientific research.

UT2 stands for *Umlauf-und-Kavitations-Tank 2* (Circulation and Cavitation Tank No. 2).

Cavitation is a phenomenon whereby the movement of a ship's propeller blades creates different kinds of bubbles underwater, whose energy, when they implode, has the potential to damage the propeller itself.

© Jacek Ruta/TU Berlin

In extreme cases, these bubbles can have the same destructive effect as a hammer on metal.

UT2 simulates real-life conditions of stress on moving propellers; it is the world's largest testing station used to study these kinds of currents.

The main pipe, in which masses of water move during experiments, runs along the ground inside the building. The surrounding walls are covered with open galleries, crowded with machines, control consoles, measuring equipment, and archive cabinets – not dissimilar to the hold of an oceanographic ship. This explains why researchers refer to different levels as 'decks' rather than 'floors'.

The circulation of water through the looped pipe (120 metres long, 19 metres high, and 8 metres in diameter) is powered by two diesel boat engines capable of carrying 3,300 tonnes of water at a flow speed ranging from 4 to 10 metres per second.

© Philipp Lohöfener

PRENZLAUER BERG

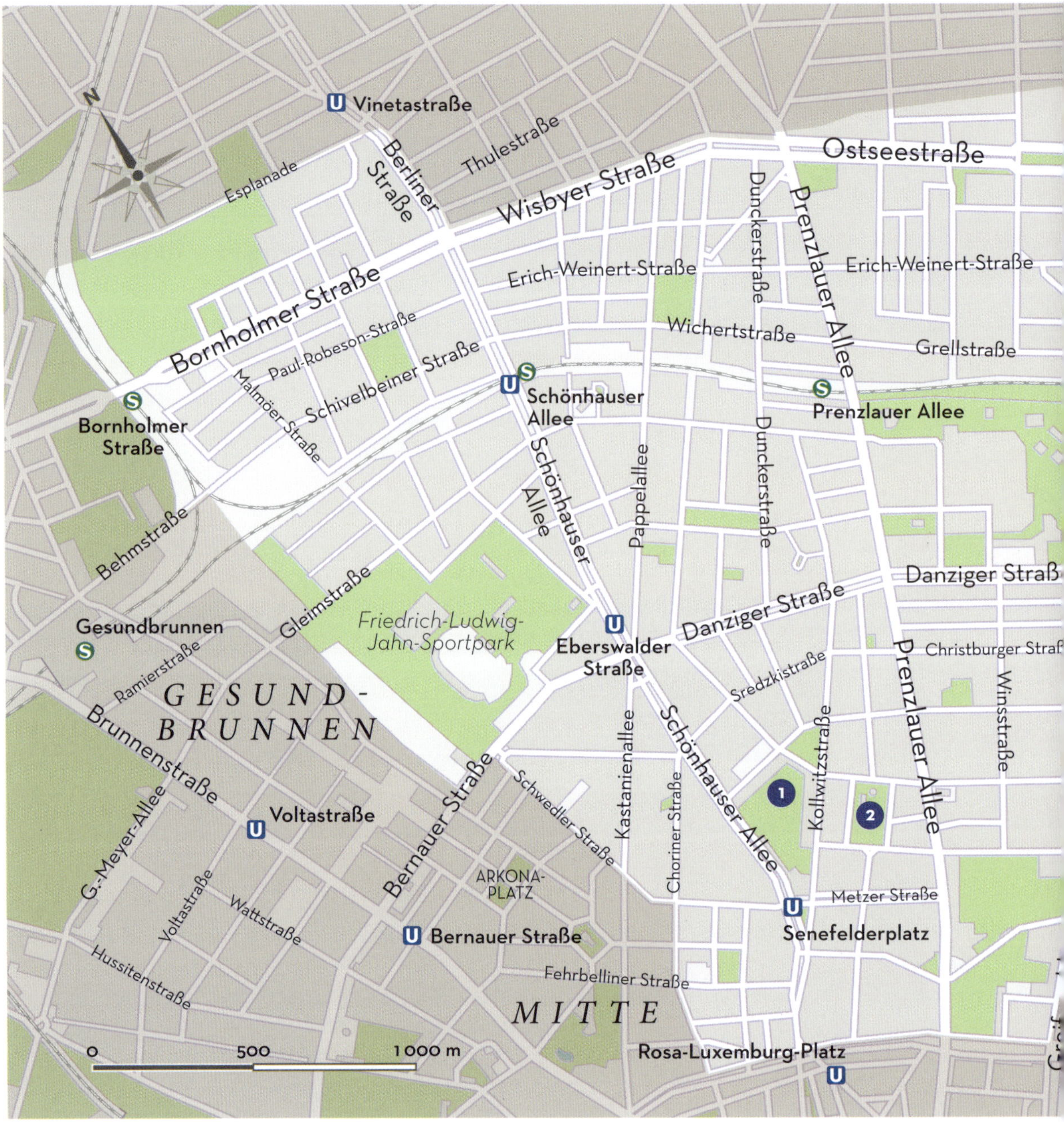

01. THE WELL IN THE JEWISH CEMETERY *p. 172*

02. THE PRENZLAUER BERG WATER TANKS *p. 176*

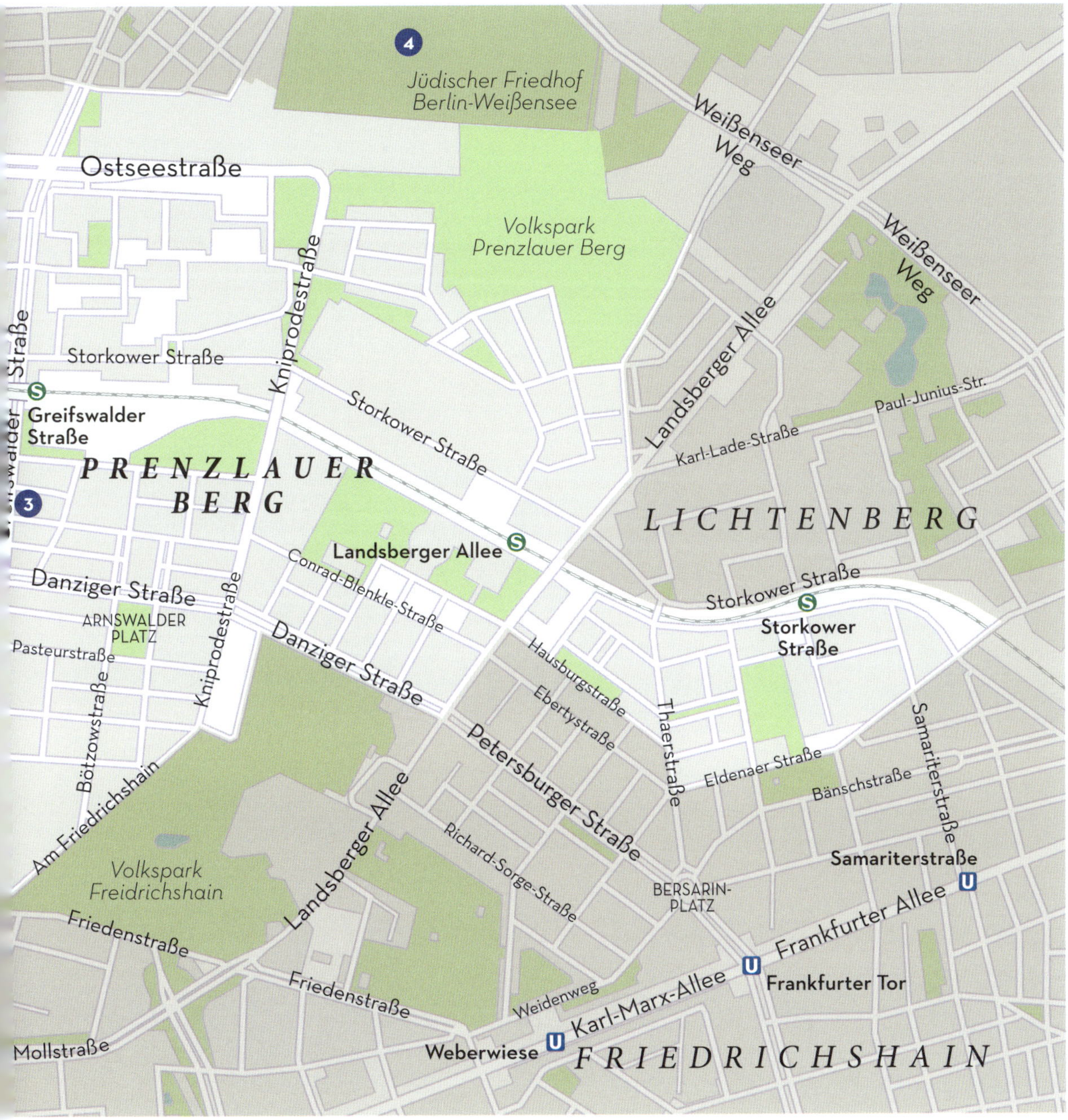

03. COAT OF ARMS OF THE GRÜNE STADT GATE *p. 182*

04. THE TOMB OF THE LEWINSOHN AND NETTER FAMILIES *p. 184*

01.

Jüdischer Friedhof Schönhauser Allee
Schönhauser Allee 23–25
U2 (Senefelderplatz)

THE WELL IN THE JEWISH CEMETERY

A well where deserters hid in 1944

In the northwest section of the Jüdischer Friedhof Schönhauser Allee (Jewish Cemetery on Schönhauser Allee), a commemorative plaque is located above a disturbing small well protected by a railing. It bears the inscription '*Den Tod anderer / nicht zu wollen / das war ihr Tod / Hier verbargen sich am Ende des / Jahres 1944 Kriegsgegner / Sie wurden von der SS entdeckt / an den Bäumen erhängt / und hier verscharrt*' ('Not wanting the death of others, they met their own death. Opponents of the war hid here at the end of 1944. They were discovered by the SS, hanged from the trees, and buried here').

This well indeed commemorates a tragic event that took place at the end of World War II: young people (whose identities and exact number are unknown) who wanted to escape the fighting decided to hide in an underground cistern of the old brewery that stood on this site in the early 19th century before giving way to the cemetery. They were discovered by the SS and hanged. Their bodies were buried on site in a mass grave. The well leads directly to the location of their hiding place. The plaque was installed after the war.

It was at the initiative of East Berlin city councilman Arnold Munter, a member of the anti-Nazi resistance who survived the Theresienstadt concentration camp, that the plaque was installed.

Founded in 1827 to compensate for the closure of the old cemetery on Große Hamburger Straße, the Jewish cemetery on Schönhauser Allee is the second-oldest Jewish cemetery in the city. In 1880, it was entirely replaced by the Weißensee cemetery, which is currently the largest in Europe. At the cemetery entrance, the Lapidarium displays more than 60 tombstones from the 19th and 20th centuries, as well as explanatory panels on Jewish funeral rites.

DEN TOD ANDERER
NICHT ZU WOLLEN
DAS WAR IHR TOD
HIER VERBARGEN SICH ENDE DES
JAHRES 1944 KRIEGSGEGNER.
SIE WURDEN VON DER SS ENTDECKT,
AN DEN BÄUMEN ERHÄNGT
UND HIER VERSCHARRT.

SYMBOLS ON JEWISH TOMBSTONES

Judaism views symbols as a representation of the bond uniting humanity with God (in contrast to 'diabolism,' which separates humanity from God). These symbols are still in use today. Here is an explanation of the most common ones:

One of Judaism's most well-known symbols – two hands in a blessing gesture with fingers spread apart – appears on the graves of members of the Cohen (or Coen) family: in Hebrew, *kohèn* means 'priest.' They thus indicate a male descendant of Aaron, Moses' brother and the first high priest of the Jewish people.

The pitcher pouring water indicates membership in the tribe of the Levites (the house of Levi), whose task in ancient times was to assist the priests during religious services by washing their hands before the blessing.

The crown, for its part, represents both political authority and the dignity displayed by the deceased. It is cited in the 'Pirkei Avot' ('Chapters of the Fathers'), one of the foundational texts of Judaism: 'There are three crowns: the crown of the Torah, the crown of the priesthood, and the crown of kingship; but the fourth crown, that of fame, surpasses them all.'

Animal figures, which appear frequently, symbolize the name of the deceased. The lion, often depicted alongside a crown, signifies not only royalty – and thus descent from the line of David – but also the given name Léon (Leo in Italian, Loeb or Loew in German).

The wolf is the emblem of the tribe of Benjamin. It refers to a surname very common in the Jewish community (Wolf in English and German, Zeev in Hebrew).

In Jewish symbolism, the deer represents the descendants of the tribe of Naphtali. It refers to the name Hirsch (in Yiddish and German), Zvi (in Hebrew), or Naftali.

Although it is one of the best-known symbols of Jewish culture and religion, the Star of David (Magen David) does not strictly speaking have a Jewish origin.

02.

Belforter Straße
U2 (Senefelderplatz)

THE PRENZLAUER BERG WATER TANKS

Remnants of the city's old water supply network

Few Berliners know that the 20-meter-high tower on the artificial hill in Park am Wasserturm was part of the city's water supply system, which also included two spectacular reservoirs that still exist beneath the hill. Built between 1852 and 1873 in an area then known as the Windmühlenberg ('Windmill Hill'), these reservoirs can be visited by appointment.
The guided tour provides access to the Kleine Wasserspeicher ('small water reservoir'), inaugurated in 1856, which could supply drinking water to over 400,000 Berliners, as well as to the Große Wasserspeicher ('large water reservoir'), and the underground rooms of the former Brauerei Königstadt, one of the many breweries in Prenzlauer Berg in the 19th century.
Following the modernization of Berlin's water system, both reservoirs were abandoned in 1914.

Across from the square at Park am Wasserturm, the Wasserturm is an imposing 30-meter-high water tower that was completed in 1877 and remained in service until 1952. Inside, beneath the 1,200-cubic-meter reservoir, the technicians' quarters have been converted into private apartments.
The water tower's machine room, which had been converted into a concentration camp in 1933, was destroyed in 1935.

HOW DOES BERLIN GET ITS WATER?

Until the second half of the 19th century, the population was supplied with water from thousands of wells scattered throughout the city. The wells were often located a few metres from the septic tanks that contaminated them.
In 1856, water was pumped from the Spree and running water was installed: the first central water supply station was inaugurated in front of the Stralau Gate, one of the gates of the toll wall (see page 64), slightly east of the Oberbaumbrücke on the north bank of the Spree. Nothing is left of this gate. Water from the river was filtered with sand before being pumped into the town's water pipes. The system was supplemented by a water tower and a reservoir with a capacity of 3,000 m^3 located on the Windmühlenberg (Windmill Hill) in what is now the Park am Wasserturm in Prenzlauer Berg (see page 176). Originally open-air, the reservoir, which was closed over by a vaulted ceiling in 1877, is no longer visible from the outside, but the tower, known as the Steigrohrturm, is still clearly visible (not to be confused with the much wider water tower that was built later overlooking Knaakstraße, which also served as a reservoir). The reservoir met the additional demand in times of high consumption and the tower was used to regulate the pressure in the pipes.
When the Stralau station reached its maximum capacity, it was first supplemented by a new station in Tegel in 1877, and finally abandoned in 1893 in favour of the Friedrichshagen station on the banks of the Müggelsee, which was then the largest and most modern distribution station in Europe. In addition, numerous water towers were built between 1877 and 1929 to meet the needs of hospitals and factories, or the new, rapidly expanding outlying districts.
Upon the instructions of the doctor and virologist Rudolf Virshow and the engineer James Hobrecht, the sanitary issues were tackled at the same time, and an underground sewage system was installed in the city to avoid polluting the Spree and the water tables with waste water, which formed an open sewer: this water contributed greatly to the cholera and typhus epidemics that devastated the city at that time.
The sewage network, which was more than 1,200 km in length, was built between 1873 and 1909. The city was divided into 12 so-called radial districts (Radialbezirke), because their sewage systems were arranged in a star shape around the lowest point of the district, leading the district's wastewater along a natural slope (see next double page). From there, it was pumped outside the city walls by means of powerful pumps, where it was used as fertilizer for land purchased for this purpose by the city (Riesenfelder): these vegetable crops in turn fed the Berliners.
These sewage networks, which are still in use today, continued using their original pumps for a very long time.
Following Germany's reunification, the Friedrichshagen waterworks were reorganised so that all the water was drawn exclusively from groundwater. For this reason, part of the complex is no longer in operation: it houses the museum of Berlin's water management and its history. This main station was supplemented by eight other stations, which have since been modernised many times: Kaulsdorf (1916), Wuhlheide (1914), Stolpe (Brandenburg) (1911), Tegel (1877), Spandau (1897), Tiefwerder (1914), Kladow (1932/1937) and Beelitzhof (1888/1894).
Today, through 8,000 km of pipes, these nine Berlin stations deliver almost 600,000 m^3 of drinking water every day, which they draw exclusively from the Berlin groundwater through 650 wells at a depth of 30 to 170 metres.
These stations therefore no longer pump water from the Spree.
On the other hand, 164 pumping stations (compa-red to the 12 historical pumping stations of the then much smaller city) pump waste water to six sewage treatment plants in Münchehofe, Schönerlinde, Wansdorf (Brandenburg), Ruhleben, Stahnsdorf and Waßmannsdorf, where it is treated before being discharged into Berlin's watercourses – the Riesenfelder concept is no longer used.

BERLIN'S 12 HISTORIC SEWAGE PUMPING STATIONS

Radialsystem I: Reichenberger Straße 66, in Kreuzberg, opened in 1879, demolished in 1977 despite strong waves of protest (a mosaic in Reichenberger Straße recalls the blasting operation, see page 78).
Radialsystem II: Gitschiner Straße 7-11 in Kreuzberg, inaugurated in 1879 and destroyed during the Second World War. Today replaced by modern facilities still in operation.
Radialsystem III: Schöneberger Straße 21 in Kreuzberg, opened in 1877 and decommissioned in 1979. Today it houses the offices of the collector Christian Boros (owner of the Boros Sammlung in Mitte).
Radialsystem IV: Scharnhorststraße 9/10 (from 1907 Scharnhorststraße 12) in Mitte, opened in 1879. It was taken out of service in 2011, then demolished.
Radialsystem V: Holzmarktstraße 31/32 in Friedrichshain, opened in 1880 and decommissioned in 1999. Since 2005, the modernised building has housed a private institution for cultural and business events.
Radialsystem VI: Urbanstraße 177 in Kreuzberg, opened in 1885. Destroyed after it was decommissioned in 1981. The gate of the original building has been preserved and is still visible at the same address.
Radialsystem VII: Lützowstraße 46-51 (Tiergarten), opened in 1885 and decommissioned in 1982. All the buildings still exist, including one of the original pumps. Since 1988, the complex has housed a youth centre, a youth hostel and a restaurant for private events.
Radialsystem VIII: Alt-Moabit 70 / Gotzkowsky Straße 22 (Moabit), opened in 1890 and decommissioned in 1989. The original buildings now house an auditorium and sports facilities.
Radialsystem IX: Seestraße 2 (Wedding), opened in 1886 and decommissioned in 1997. The buildings were demolished in 2000. Since 1997, a modern pumping station has replaced the old one.
Radialsystem X: Bellermannstraße 7 (Gesundbrunnen), opened in 1890.
Radialsystem XI: Erich-Weinert-Straße 131 (Prenzlauer Berg), opened in 1909 and decommissioned in 2002. Behind the magnificent period buildings there is now a modern pump that has replaced the original one.
Radialsystem XII: Rudolfstraße 15 (Friedrichshain), opened in 1893, the pump was modernised in the 1910s and 1930s and is still in operation today (it has been twinned with another modern pump station since 1999).

03.

Greifswalder Straße 55–56
S 8, 41, 42, 85 (Greifswalder Straße)

COAT OF ARMS OF THE GRÜNE STADT GATE

A tribute to tradesmen

Between numbers 55 and 56 of Greifswalderstraße in Prenzlauer Berg is a large vaulted entrance flanked by two gates that leads to the inner courtyards of the Grüne Stadt (Green City). This former municipal social housing complex was built in 1938-39 by architect Werner Harding and later privatised in 2004. The dwellings were intended for the working-class population – the gate bears witness to this.
In contrast to the building's façades – a simple plaster coating exempt of decoration – the portal, with its red terracotta tiles, is bordered by a frieze etched in stucco, composed of interlace patterns and coats of arms. Painted in black and white on a red background, these coats of arms are a collection of emblems (in some cases dating back to the Middle Ages) representing traditionally manual trades, a tribute to the working-class populations who lived here.

Above the door on the left is the emblem of the rope makers; it comprises the heart, anchor, rake (used to guide the ropes while they are being braided), and hooks with hand cranks (operated in order to braid rope).
Above the door on the right is the emblem of the brewers, which features a ladle, shovel, ears of wheat, and hops.
From left to right around the large vaulted entrance are the emblems of many more trades: locksmiths (keys and a cogwheel); engineers (compass, pickaxe and hammer); roofers (compass, hammer and pointed hammer); glaziers (glass-cutting diamond (horizontal), sledgehammer (vertical), hammer, and soldering iron); carpenters (compass, tri-square and rebate plane); tailors (needle, scissors and triangular protractor); house painters (imperial eagle and a shield marked with three small coats of arms); chimney sweepers (shovels and a small brush); stonecutters (a stonecutter's monogram – a signature with which the sculptors once marked every one of their stones); potters (potter's wheel flanked by flames and the letters T and O, probably for Töpfer-Orden – the Craft Potters Association); carpenters (axe, tri-square and whipsaw – a saw with two handles, in this case attached to a pendulum); and woodworkers

(scissors and a poorly drawn compass).
On the left inside the vaulted passage is the blacksmiths' emblem (a horseshoe), while on the right is the electricians' emblem, featuring a lightning bolt crossed by electrical wires and three disconnectors (a type of high-voltage switch).
From the courtyard above the left door is another depiction of the carpenters' emblem, while on the cornerstone is the masons' emblem, composed of compass, pickaxe, angle, and shovel.
Lastly, from the courtyard above the door on the right, is another ropemaker's emblem.

04.

Jewish cemetery of Berlin-Weißensee
Herbert-Baum-Straße 45
S8, 41, 42, 85 (Greifswalder Straße),
then Tram M1, 4, 13 (Albertinenstraße)

THE TOMB OF THE LEWINSOHN AND NETTER FAMILIES

An exceptional tomb

In the heart of the magnificent Jewish cemetery of Berlin-Weißensee (perhaps one of the most beautiful cemeteries in Europe), it is easy to miss some of the beautiful graves and the quality of their features, as there are so many of them. The most beautiful one is a real gem that must not be missed. In order to find it, you should ask for a plan at the entrance and look for the plot at the junction of the paths IIA, IIB, IIG and IIH. Almost exactly at the junction of these four paths, the tomb of the Lewinsohn and Netter families is surrounded by a spectacular cast iron fence, decorated with dozens of golden flowers, entwined with green leaves and a burgundy red-coloured motif on the flower buds and on some of the leaves. Designed in 1893 by Fabian, the tomb houses four sarcophagi with plaques bearing the dates of birth and death of the deceased who passed away between 1893 and 1922. The tomb was restored between 2000 and 2002 with money from the historical monuments fund of the Land of Berlin.

Not to be missed either is the intersection of the paths IIK, IIJ, IIR and IIS: all the tombs in this little square are exceptional. Of particular interest are the tombs of the Adam, Friedlaender and Baszynski families, of Art Nouveau inspiration.

FRIEDRICHSHAIN – RUMMELSBURG

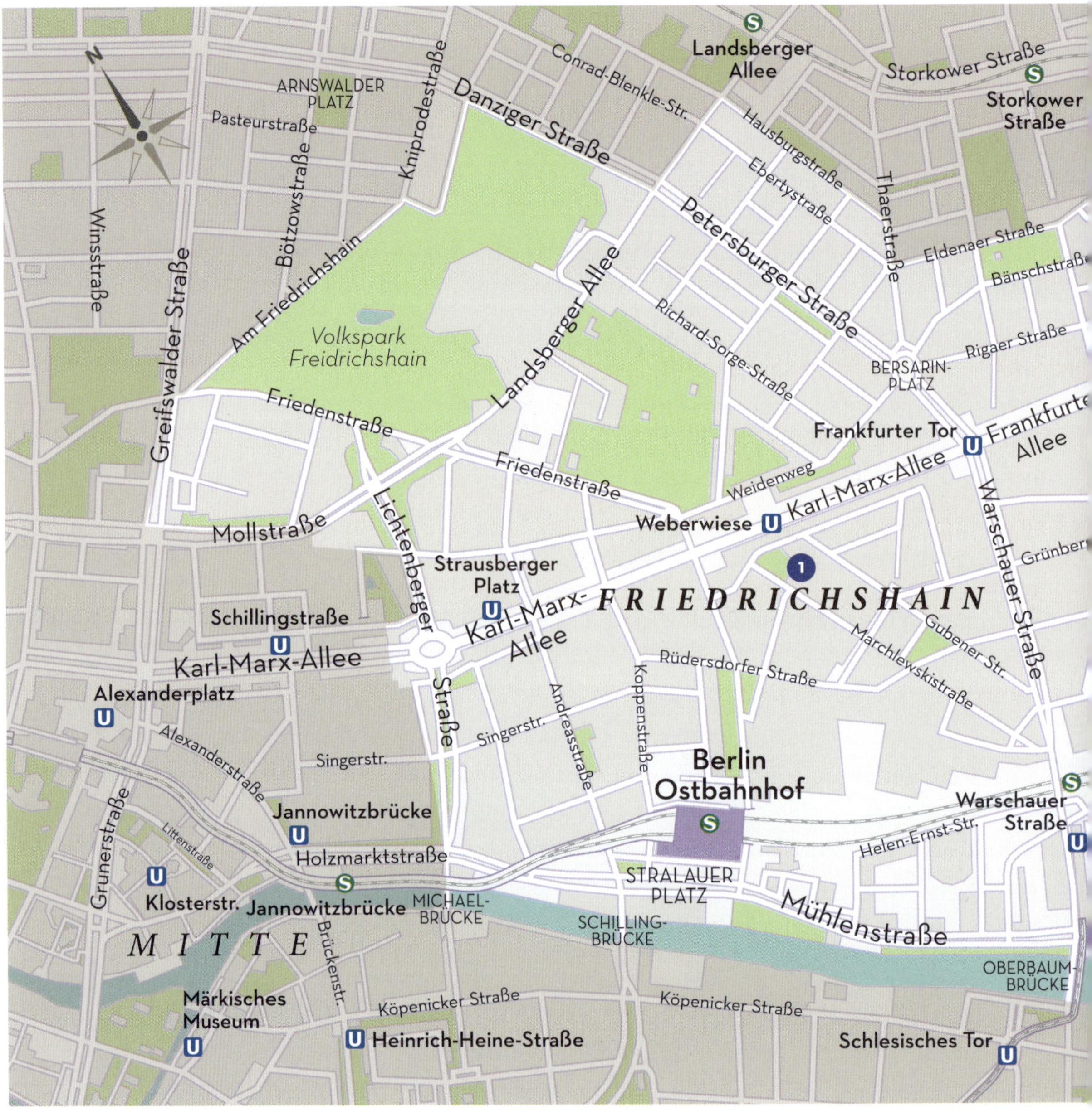

01. THE COLUMNS OF WEBERWIESE *p. 188*

02. LEANING TOWER OF STRALAU CHURCH *p. 190*

LICHTENBERG
RUMMELSBURG
Lichtenberg
Einbecker Straße
Magdalenenstraße
Frankfurter Allee
Möllendorffstraße
Buchberger Str.
Margaretenstr.
Marie-Curie-Allee
Weitlingstraße
Pettenkoferstraße
Samariterstraße
Bänschstr.
Rigaer Straße
Samariterstraße
Schulze-Boysen-Straße
Scharnweberstraße
Gürtelstraße
Münsterlandstr.
Nöldnerplatz
Lückstraße
Boxhagener-Straße
Weserstraße
Kaskelstraße
Nöldnerstr.
Wühlischstraße
Marktstr.
Simplonstraße
Rummelsburg
Hauptstraße
Ostkreuz
Hauptstraße
Modersohnstraße
Markgrafendam
Kynaststraße
Rummelsburger see
Rotherstraße
Corinthstraße
Fischzug
Stralauer Allee
Alt-Stralau
2
Spree
ELSEN-BRÜCKE
Treptower Park
Treptower Park
0
500
1000 m

01.

Marchlewskistraße 25
U5 (Weberwiese)

THE COLUMNS OF WEBERWIESE

Columns that come from Göring's mansion

Built in just a year, between 1951 and 1952, by the architect Hermann Henselmann, the famous tower of Weberwiese was the first high-rise tower block to be built in post-war East Berlin. Very few Berliners, or even inhabitants of the tower block, are aware that the remains of an old, private Nazi mansion were used to build this neoclassical construction. The dark black-green columns of polished dolerite at the entrance of the building, in addition to the material used in the main entrance hall up to the foot of the stairs, do indeed come from Carinhall, Göring's country estate north-east of Berlin.

At the beginning of the 1940s, the columns were used to decorate the enlargement of Carinhall, which was the country retreat of Reichsmarschall Göring, built as a northern-style wooden house on the banks of the Wuckersee lake, in the forest of Schorfheide. This enormous new building was built to house Göring's looted private art collection. Göring (who also owned another chalet near Hitler's Berghof in the Bavarian Alps) had Carinhall demolished when the war was coming to an end as he was afraid that his property would fall into the hands of the Allies. Some of the confiscated and stolen paintings, which he wrongly considered to be worthless, were burnt. The ruins were removed at the time of the GDR, and today there is nothing left but a bunker full of random waste, which regularly attracts treasure hunters.

Built mainly with bricks found in the rubble after the bombings, the tower block was fitted with an outer cladding in Meißen ceramic (not porcelain!) – supplied by the long-established factory, founded by Carl Teicher in Meißen, which produced tiling for stoves and buildings.

Applying the principles of the training that he had received, Henselmann initially designed the building in the modern pre-war architectural style, but his initial design was rejected. This piece of socialist realism was therefore built instead, which, strangely enough, meant that Nazi neoclassicism was upheld in the east. This building was to inaugurate the national reconstruction plan for the entire newly-established GDR, and serve as a model for the planned Stalinallee. It proved to be so costly that the building alone was to embody the whole economic concept of the GDR, namely to take advantage of generous state subsidies to impress the crowds. Until 1989, an apartment in this building cost only a ninth of what would have been needed to cover the building and maintenance costs.

02.

Tunnelstraße 5–11
S8, 9, 41, 42 (Treptower Park) / S3, 5, 7, 8, 9, 41, 42 (Ostkreuz), then Bus 347

LEANING TOWER OF STRALAU CHURCH

A tower more inclined than the Tower of Pisa?

Shortly before the tip of the charming Stralau peninsula is a small 15th-century church. Its white tower – a much later addition – is actually leaning more steeply than the Tower of Pisa. While its Italian counterpart slopes 3.9 degrees to the south, the Kirchturm Stralau is said to slope 5 degrees to the north-west. In this case, the church in Stralau would have one of the most steeply inclined towers in the world.

According to some sources, the tower is said to have buckled as a result of damage during the Second World War.

On 26 February 1945 the church was hit by a bomb that destroyed the entire nave vault. When the church was rebuilt at the end of the 1950s, it was said that the crater left by the bomb was badly filled in, which then led to subsidence of the ground and the inclination of the tower.

However, further research has shown that this inclination had been observed as early as 1934 – two windows of the nave of Stralau Church still have their original stained glass.

The cemetery located next to the church is a remarkable place to spend a quiet moment; the slope of the embankment overlooking the Spree is an ideal spot to rest and listen to the sound of water splashing along the bank.

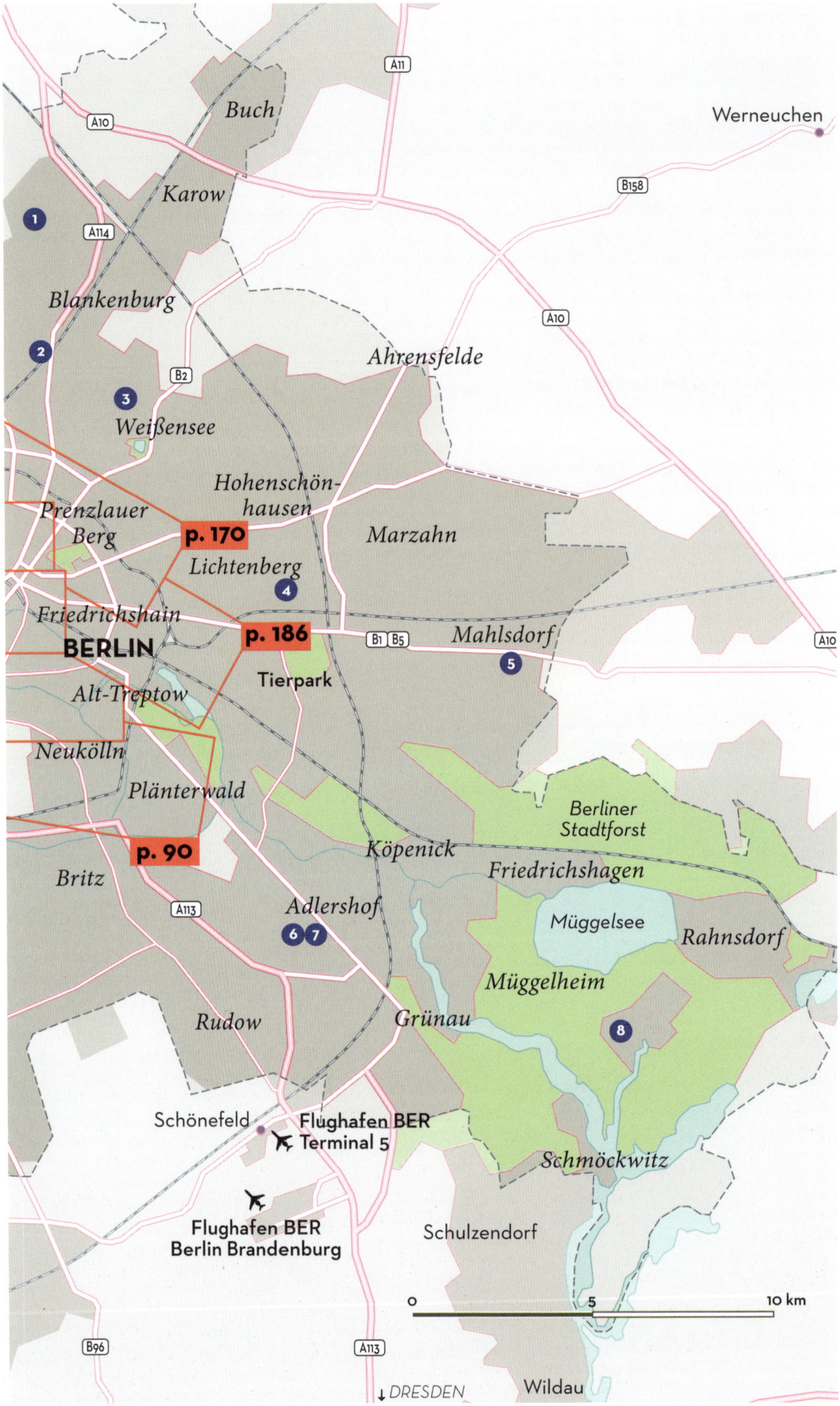
A11
A10
Buch
Werneuchen
B158
Karow
1
A114
Blankenburg
A10
2
B2
Ahrensfelde
3
Weißensee
Hohenschön-
hausen
Prenzlauer
Berg
p. 170
Marzahn
Lichtenberg
4
Friedrichshain
p. 186
B1 B5
Mahlsdorf
A10
BERLIN
5
Tierpark
Alt-Treptow
Neukölln
Plänterwald
Berliner
Stadtforst
Köpenick
p. 90
Friedrichshagen
Britz
A113
Adlershof
Müggelsee
Rahnsdorf
6 7
Müggelheim
Rudow
Grünau
8
Schönefeld
Flughafen BER
Terminal 5
Schmöckwitz
Flughafen BER
Berlin Brandenburg
Schulzendorf
0
5
10 km
B96
A113
DRESDEN
Wildau

PANKOW – LICHTENBERG – TREPTOW-KÖPENICK

01.

Botanischer Volkspark
Blankenfelder Chaussee 5
geowand.gruen-berlin.de (interactive geological wall)
Bus 107 (Botanischer Volkspark)

GEOLOGICAL WALL

A major geological attraction

With its many numbered stones scattered here and there, the long wall of natural stones at the farthest corner of the Botanischer Volkspark seems to have been erected by an overly enthusiastic landscape gardener. Built between 1891 and 1896, this wall is in fact a major geological attraction and a historical curiosity in the city of Berlin; it has recently been ranked 78th 'national geotope'.

Eduard Zache (1862-1929), a member of the German Geological Society and the Brandenburgia History Society, was the man behind this 'geological wall'. The wall was originally located in Humboldthain Park, which used to be a botanical and geological garden for educational purposes in memory of Alexander von Humboldt.

In 1909 the central pedagogical garden on the road to Blankenfelde (the current botanical park) was entrusted with this educational mission as part of a broader scientific aim. The geological wall of Dr Zache (PhD and professor at Andreas High School on Koppensstraße) was therefore also transferred to this new site.

The 30-metre-long and 2.5-metre-high wall reproduced an ideal cross-section through the geological history of Central Europe. Divided into 20 parts, it is comprised of 123 types of stone, minerals, earth, and ore from Brandenberg, the Rhine region, Silesia, Saxony, and Thuringia.

Starting on the left, where the most recent sediments are located, and moving right, the layers date back in time. At the end are the oldest rocks of the crystalline basement.

In reality, these strata are laid out vertically from top to bottom. However, to make the presentation of this structure easier, and the wall relatively small, Dr Zache inserted faults between the layers (which should be imagined as vertical fractures) that constitute the canals along which magma travels to reach the surface, as well as fold formations that disrupt the chronological order of the strata. Minerals and fossils are incorporated in several places.

Flying over the wall from left to right, a bird would cross 300 million years of our geological era in no time at all.

52
53
51
55
54
49
48
47
41
38

02.

Breite Straße 45
Tram 50 (Pankow Kirche)

THE CHERUBS OF PANKOW

Each angel represents a type of human temperament

A few metres from the tram tracks at Breite Strasse 45, four small stone angels stand on stelae. These four sculptures are copies of the originals (part of the sculpture collections of the Berlin State Museums since 1962, where they are protected from pollution) by the famous sculptor Gottfried Knöffler (1715-1779). They represent the four types of human temperament as described by Hippocrates:

The choleric character, angry and enraged, even though his more troubling problem is being in the mouth of a fire-breathing dragon.

Beside the angel (his symbol), the spirited and fiery sanguine character makes overly ambitious plans from atop his cumulus.

Leaning on his spade as if it were a pilgrim's staff, his hands tied, the phlegmatic character will not waste an ounce of energy on unnecessary labour.

The melancholic character casts a dubious glance at a book (perhaps the Bible) without reading it. He spends his life worrying, ends up feeling sorry for himself, and withdraws from the world.

Built in 1770, this single-storey building, called Kavalierhaus (the equivalent of a castle's communal area), was in fact just a simple country house. It never belonged to any member of the court, but to merchants such as Carl Philipp Möring (1753-1837), who in 1814 had one of Germany's first steam boilers installed in the orangery; and Charles Duvinage (1804-1871), who established the Hohenzollern library.

From 1866 to 1939 the house was owned by the family of the chocolate manufacturer Richard Hildebrand. From 1947 onwards the building was used by the Great Berlin Social Welfare Office, before it became a school day care centre in 1953.

In 1998 the Caritas-Krankenhilfe Berlin e.V. acquired the building and renovated it in accordance with the regulations for the preservation of historical monuments.

03.

An der Industriebahn 12
S8, 41, 42 (Greifswalder Straße)
then bus 225 (Roelckestraße/Nüßlerstraße)

THE PAINTER OF THE MOTORWERK

A discreet tribute to an 'industrial painter'

In the industrial wasteland that once incorporated the Weißensee railway junction, to the left of the entrance to the former long production hall of Ziehl-Abegg, stands a rather surprising work of art: an enigmatic bespectacled dwarf poses with his arms behind his back next to what was once the company's flagship product — an electric motor with an external rotor.

Anyone with an interest in Berlin's 19th-century art history will immediately recognise the caricatured man; the white beard covering chin and cheeks, the silhouette and oversized head barely poking out above the motor, and the look of eternal grumpiness all belong to Adolph von Menzel (1815-1905), a Prussian historian and the first 'industrial painter'. His best known painting, 'Das Eisenwalzwerk' ('The Iron Rolling Mill'), completed between 1872-75, is hanging in the Alte Nationalgalerie.

Emil Ziehl (1873-1939), the founder of the Ziehl-Abegg company, was a gifted artist, and even wanted to become a painter for a while. His fascination for engineering gradually took over, but he continued to draw for pleasure. So when the time came to think about a work of art for his new factory, he made a whimsical sketch in homage to the first Berlin painter who had drawn inspiration from industry. The drawing is symbolic of modernism catching up and taking over the 'spirit' of fin-de-siècle.

On the same wall, an advertisement also shows Ziehl's caricature of old Menzel standing in front of the Ziehl-Abegg external rotor electric motor. After Bruno Buch and Karl Herrmann built the production hall for the Ziehl-Abegg electricity company at the beginning of the 1920s, the Motorwerk site became a venue for events.

04.

Am Tierpark 125
U5 (Tierpark)

FOUR BRONZE LIONS OF THE TIERPARK

One of the rare remains of the William I National Monument

Four gigantic bronze lions stand guard in front of the feline enclosure in Berlin's Tierpark (the former East Berlin Zoo). Together with the imperial eagle in the Märkisches Museum and the original pedestal, these sculptures are among the few remains of the Wilhelm I National Monument, which stood on the banks of the River Spree in front of Berlin Castle until 1950.

During his reign, William I managed to politically unify the Germanic countries around the Hohenzollern dynasty, raising Germany to the status of an almost invincible power. Inaugurated in 1897, some ten years after his death, the William I National Monument celebrated what would soon become Europe's nightmare. Four lions, figures of nobility and domination, stood at the corners of the memorial facing the four cardinal points. Seeing it as a symbol of Prussian militarism, the East German regime had the monument dismantled and liquidated together with Hohenzollern Castle in 1950, a few months after the founding of the GDR. Deprived of the Zoological Gardens, East Berlin decided to buy a zoo, and the lions that had been stored in the Museum of the History of the Old Arsenal (at Unter den Linden 2) were brought out.

How was it then that the GDR looked favourably upon these lions (along with the eagle in the Märkisches Museum)? They had in fact been modelled by internationally renowned animal sculptor August Gaul, who had joined the Berlin Secession, a movement that revolved around painter Max Liebermann and gallery owner and publisher Paul Cassirer, both intellectuals who played a decisive role in the development of modern art in Germany, which was abhorred by the Nazis.

05.

Adlershof Aerodynamic Park
Brook-Taylor-Straße 2
Tram 60, 61, 63 (Karl-Ziegler-Straße)

TRUDELTURM VERTICAL WIND TUNNEL

A concrete egg to study spinning

Though far from the city centre, the Adlershof aerodynamic park – located on the site of the Deutsches Zentrums für Luft und Raumfahrt (German Aerospace Centre) – should be on every architecture enthusiast's list of places to visit.

Surrounded by the district's modern university buildings, the centre comprises three exceptional buildings from the 1930s, the era of pioneering aeronautical research.

Among the three is the large wind tunnel where the aerodynamics of the world's largest fighter aircraft, the Messerschmitt ME 262, were apparently optimised. It still seems to be operational and has been used several times as a location for science fiction films; the former aircraft engine test bench, with its large chimneys in the shape of exhaust pipes, has been converted into a cafeteria; and the enigmatic Trudelturm, the wind tunnel tower for spinning tests.

Evoking a high-rise dwelling on the planet Mars, the Trudelturm resembles a giant concrete pear with a single door almost halfway up, which is accessed by an external staircase that follows the building's curvature.

Once inside, the impression of being in a turbine is striking. A large concrete ring runs around the wall above visitors' heads; this is where simulations were carried out using model aircrafts to study the dreaded spin phenomenon, which was still relatively unknown in 1936.

The wind generator built into the ground projected a powerful upward flow of air. From these experiments, techniques were developed that helped enable pilots to prevent spins when an aircraft stalled and tilted, or to quickly and safely stop a flat or steep spin, regardless of the direction of rotation.

It is possible to view a film online that was made back in the day for the DVL (Deutsche Versuchsanstalt für Luftfahrt – the German Aeronautical Research Centre) showing a simulation in the vertical wind tunnel. The film is entitled 'Maßnahmen zum Beenden des Abkippens und Trudelns' (1941), which translates as 'Recommendations for recovering from a stall and a spin'.

Located nearby, the former Berlin-Johannisthal airfield has become an astonishing and beautiful protected natural area. It would be a pity not to visit it after the aeronautical park.

06.

Zum Schmetterlingshorst 2
Tram 62 (Wendenschloss)

THE SCHMETTERLINGSHORST BUTTERFLY COLLECTION

Butterfly hunting in the Köpenick forest

Opposite Grünau beach, on the north bank of the Langer See, the Schmetterlingshorst (also a base for the Treptow-Köpenick District Sports Association) offers a pleasant terrace for a quiet drink, though few guests believe that the name of the place (*Schmetterling* in German means 'butterfly') still has any significance. However, the central building houses a remarkable collection of butterflies and insects, some of which are rather frightening. In total there are 3,150 butterflies spanning 1,250 varieties, along with 870 other insects, some of which are rare specimens of species that have already disappeared.

This world-class collection (the largest of its kind in Germany and the second largest in Europe) originated in the early 20th century.

Johann Bittner, a master glass engraver originating from Bohemia, had set up his small refreshment bar here.

The honourable 'Circle of Lepidopterists* Orion' (founded on 1 August 1890) soon made the bar its official inn and a starting point for excursions through the Köpenick Forest. The hostel rapidly grew in popularity and was the natural choice to host the collection that Herbert Jacobs, one of the members of the Orion association, had built up between 1902 and 1952.

** Butterfly collectors*

07.

Am Studio 1A
Tram M17, 61 (Walther-Nernst-Str.)

THE ISOTHERMAL SPHERICAL LABORATORIES

An exceptional architectural surprise

Hidden among soulless modern buildings, the Isothermische Kugellabore (literally 'isothermal spherical laboratories') remain a striking surprise for the few visitors who venture into the Adlershof district.
They represent a remarkable example of 20th century experimental scientific architecture, in which the shape of the building is directly determined by a physical requirement: extreme temperature control.
Built between 1959 and 1961 in Berlin-Adlershof, these laboratories were designed for the Institute of Physical Chemistry of the Academy of Sciences of the GDR.
Initiated by the chemist Peter Adolf Thiessen, the project was carried out by the architect Horst Welser. Their aim was to enable thermochemical experiments of exceptional precision, particularly in the fields of metallurgy and aeronautical research.

The uniqueness of this complex lies in the spherical shape of the buildings: in physics, a sphere has the smallest surface area for a given volume, thereby reducing heat exchange with the environment. This architectural choice made it possible to achieve exceptional thermal stability, with temperature variations as low as 0.01°C.
The architectural structure is particularly sophisticated. Each sphere consists of several layers: a concrete shell, thick thermal insulation (in some places exceeding one metre), and an aluminium envelope. The entire system is designed to minimise heat loss.
Inside, a system combining heating, cooling and ventilation ensured precise temperature regulation.
Over time, advances in technology and evolving research needs rendered these structures obsolete. They were partially abandoned or repurposed, before eventually being protected as historic monuments.

08.

Alt-Müggelheim median strip
Alt-Müggelheim bus stop

THE JOHANN JACOB BAEYER MEMORIAL

In memory of an exceptional geographer, born in Müggelheim

At the far end of the Große Krampe, whether arriving by boat or bicycle, at the eastern edge of Müggelheim's Dorffanger, a monument topped by a striking globe commemorates Johann Jacob Baeyer (1794–1885).
In 1962, on the occasion of the centenary of the International Earth Measurement, his native village of Müggelheim, in collaboration with the Geodetic Institute of Potsdam, erected this commemorative stele close to the site of his parents' house, which was destroyed during the Second World War. The inscription reads: 'To the founder of the International Earth Measurements – 1794–1885 – Johann Jacob Baeyer – of Müggelheim – on the occasion of the 100th anniversary of the International Earth Measurement in 1962.'
During his years as an officer in the Prussian army, Baeyer carried out significant topographical work in East Prussia with the astronomer Bessel between 1831 and 1836. In 1848, he became Royal Director of the Prussian Telegraph. Appointed head of the trigonometric division of the General Staff, Baeyer left the army with the rank of lieutenant general in 1857. In 1858, he was commissioned by Prussia to conduct geodetic surveys in Central Europe, studying, among other things, the Earth's gravitational field and curvature. In 1861, he proposed a geodetic survey on a Central European scale, to which all European states (with the exception of England) agreed, turning his proposal into a European project, formalised at a conference he organised in 1862. Considered the founder of the International Association of Geodesy, established in 1864 under the name Mitteleuropäische Gradmessung (Association for the Measurement of Degrees in Central Europe), Baeyer also served as director of the Berlin Geodetic Institute, founded in 1869, until his death. In 1886, the institute moved to Potsdam on the Telegrafenberg (see the guide *Secret Potsdam* by the same publisher).

© Agadez

In Müggelheim, Johann-Jacob-Baeyer-Straße has borne this name since 1994. In 1997, Baeyer also gave his name to Baeyer Canyon, a deep-water trench in the Lazarev Sea in Antarctica. Johann Jacob Baeyer was the father of the Nobel Prize in Chemistry laureate Adolf von Baeyer.

Dem Begründer der
Internationalen Erdmessung
1794
1885
JOHANN JACOB BAEYER
aus
Müggelheim
anläßlich des 100-jährigen Bestehens
der internationalen Erdmessung
im Jahre 1962

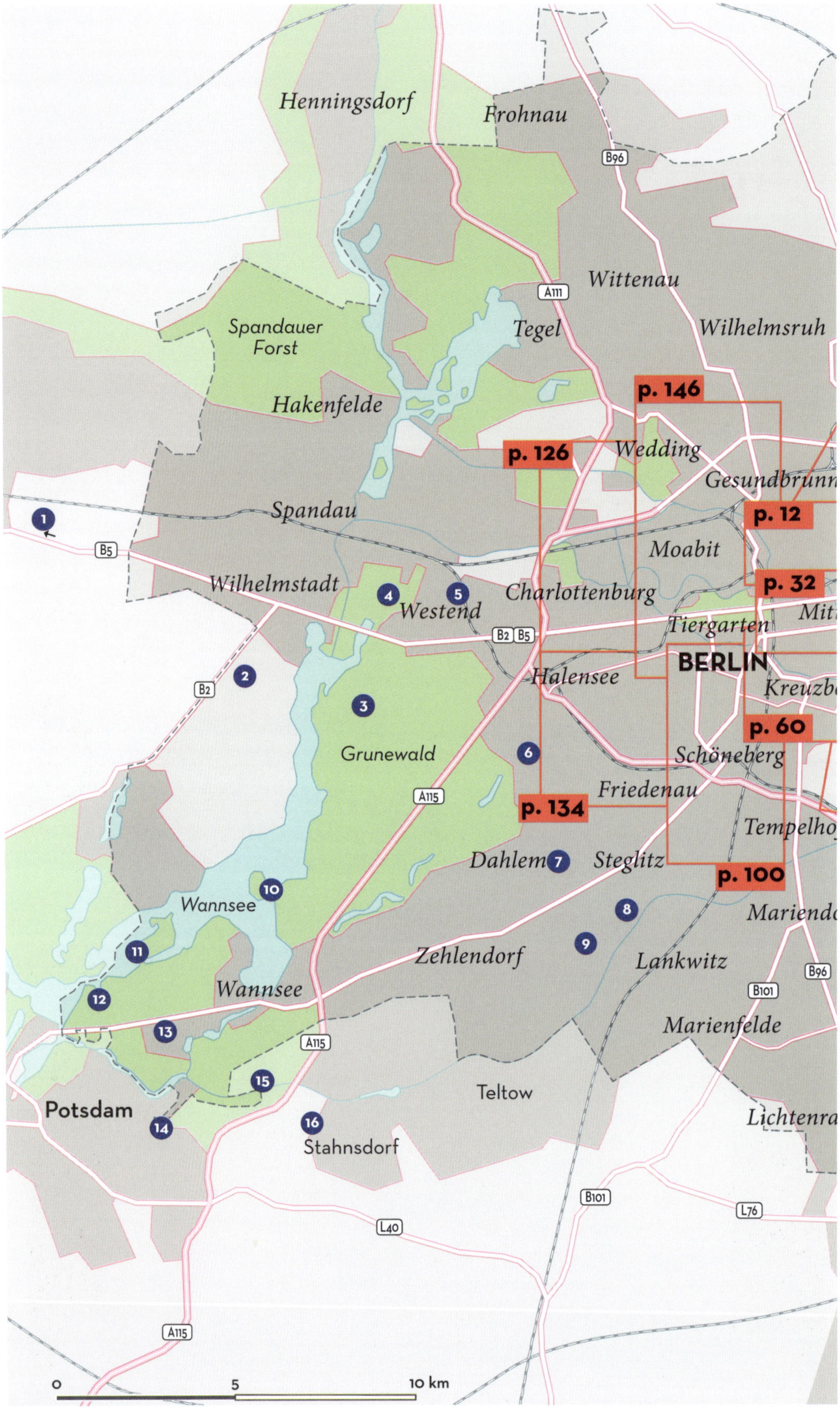
Henningsdorf
Frohnau
B96
Wittenau
A111
Tegel
Wilhelmsruh
Spandauer
Forst
Hakenfelde
p. 146
p. 126
Wedding
Gesundbrunn
Spandau
p. 12
1
B5
Moabit
p. 32
Wilhelmstadt
4
5
Westend
Charlottenburg
Tiergarten
B2
B5
2
B2
BERLIN
Halensee
Kreuzb
3
p. 60
Grunewald
6
Schöneberg
A115
Friedenau
p. 134
Tempelho
Dahlem
7
Steglitz
p. 100
10
Wannsee
8
Mariend
11
9
Zehlendorf
Lankwitz
B96
12
Wannsee
B101
13
Marienfelde
A115
15
Teltow
Potsdam
14
16
Lichtenra
Stahnsdorf
B101
L76
L40
A115
0
5
10 km

SPANDAU – GRUNEWALD – STEGLITZ-ZEHLENDORF – SCHMARGENDORF – STAHNSDORF

01.

Am Zeppelinpark 27
S3, 9 / U7 (Rathaus Spandau)
then bus M32 (Heerstraße/Nennhauser Damm)

STAAKENS'S OLD CONTROL TOWER

A forgotten witness to the heyday of zeppelins in Staaken

At the end of Brunsbütteler Damm in Staaken, on Berlin's north west border, in a bland industrial zone, the old tarmac of Staaken's airfield (1915-1953) is now covered with rows of solar panels.

Even the locals have forgotten that, up to 1918, 12 airships were built in Staaken and some parts of the production hangar are still standing today. However, everything that remains is either hidden or in ruins (or both), and there are no signs telling the history of the place.

The most visible remains are those of the old brick control tower from the 1920s, a time when Staaken was a playground for many of Berlin's well-known characters who had obtained their pilot's licence, like Wernher von Braun, Heinz Rühmann (the actor in the propoganda comedy 'Quax, der Bruchpilot'), Elli Beinhorn (the future wife of the racing driver Bernd Rosemeyer), Hanna Reitsch (the woman who conducted test flights of the V1 for Hitler) and the ill-fated Marga von Etzdorf from Spandau who, in spite of her successes at international flying competitions, committed suicide in 1933 after making two emergency crash landings.

It was in front of this rather ordinary control tower that Hitler admitted in public that he had not respected the Treaty of Versailles: by stationing all the airships at this place – Arodo Ar 65 biplanes – from the Richthofen fighter squadron, he admitted that the German Reich was building an air force.

It was also in front of this very same control tower that the first German transatlantic passenger airship was to take off: an Fw 200 V1 made by the aeronautics manufacturer Focke-Wulf – Lufthansa's D-ACON- registered Condor which flew, non-stop, to New York in a little over 24 hours, thanks to its reserve tanks.

Even faster on the return flight, it covered a distance of 6,392 kilometres in 19 hours and 55 minutes, which corresponded to an average speed of 321 km/h.

On the control tower, there is an inscription in Cyrillic characters testifying to the airport's last phase of use. The Russians moved out in 1953, leaving the airfield to its fate and closure in 1959.

02.

At the junction of Gatower Straße and Straße 270
S3, 5, 9 (Pichelsberg) then 15 min by bicycle

THE FIELDS OF KAROLINENHÖHE

A magnificent relic of the history of the drains of Berlin

To the west of the tower of Beringer, level with the right angle formed by the border between Berlin and Brandenburg, a surprising and immense area of countryside begins. By bicycle, this particularly pleasant ride takes you, for example, from the fort of Hahneberg to the Havel. The dirt tracks, installed on a sort of dyke between the fields, feel almost like ancient rice fields. These fields, called Karolinenhöhe, are actually a magnificent relic of the so-called drainage fields (Rieselfelder) which were used in Berlin for more than a century to deal with the problem of sewage. Originally belonging to the autonomous town of Charlottenburg, the Rieselfelder Karolinenhöhe were made into a protected green area covering 220 hectares in 1987. The sewage treatment plants are relatively recent: in Berlin they have only really been in use since the end of the 1960s. Before then, sewage from the capital was taken to different pumping stations, which evacuated them out of the town using underground pressure pipes to some 20 drainage fields (Rieselfelder) covering up to 10,000 hectares of land (Karolinenhöhe, Wansdorf, Schönerlinde, Blankenfelde, Buch, Hobrechtsfelde, Malchow, Falkenberg, Hellersdorf, Münchehofe, Deutsch Wusterhausen, Kleinziethen, Großziethen, Boddinsfelde, Tasdorf, Mühlenbeck, Waßmanndorf, Osdorf, Großbeeren, Sputendorf).

Filtered naturally, the sediments were used for market gardening to feed the city of Berlin. The history of these fields goes back to the advent of running water around the end of the 19th century: before it was installed, dry toilets could be found in interior courtyards. Once full, the septic tanks were emptied at night by the Eimer-Weiber (bucket women), who carried the contents, by cart, outside the city. As for the sewage, it was thrown into the gutters (Rinnsteine). Placed between the pavement and the road, they formed a small rut, the width of a paving stone, filled with repulsive trickles of matter which flowed into the Spree.

With the arrival of running water, which also supplied enough water to rinse out the gutters, the dirty waters became mixed with the excrement from the toilets and also flowed into the gutters which lined the pavements, forming an open sewer throughout the city streets, the repulsive streams of which not only polluted the Spree but also soaked into the ground and down to the water table. The underground drainage network, with its pumping stations (see page 180) and the system of the Rieselfelfer, helped to solve this problem.

03.

Schildhornweg 33, Im Jagen 35
S3, 9 (Pichelsberg)

THE CEMETERY OF THE FOREST OF GRUNEWALD

The most mysterious, moving and poetic of cemeteries in Berlin

Of all the cemeteries in Berlin, the rarely visited cemetery of the forest of Grunewald is probably the most mysterious, moving and poetic.

Its unusual location is due to its history: it was originally reserved for those who could not be given a burial in the parish cemeteries of the town. This was either because they had committed suicide or because they had been found on the shores of the Jürgenlanke, a small, nearby bay, and they had to be buried quickly. In 1920, when the management of the cemetery was handed over to the town, those who had committed suicide were given the right to a Christian burial.

Although, in the cemetery, there are two Russian Orthodox crosses dating back to the First World War (two forced labourers who committed suicide), a significant number of graves belonging to soldiers from the Second World War, some crosses for unnamed graves, and many very 'ordinary' tombstones, three of the graves stand out from the rest. The first one belongs to Willi Wohlberedt, an author who had carried out research on cemeteries which were represented on the cover of his most important work: The tombstones of Greater Berlin, Potsdam and its surroundings. The tombstone of Willi Schulz, former inspector of the forest of Grunewald, is made up of three wooden planks standing side by side to form a tombstone. They are covered by small, pointed copper caps which come together to form the letter W for Willi in an Expressionist-style zigzag. On the right-hand and left-hand planks, a large cross has been carved into the wood; his name and title are engraved on the one in the middle, the largest of the three. Above the epitaph a deer's antlers have been fixed as a hunting trophy. Below the epitaph the sarcastic comment, 'End of the hunting season!' has been added.

The most surprising tombstone belongs to Margarethe Päffgen and her daughter Christa Päffgen, alias Nico – a former experimental rock singer with the group Velvet Underground, Andy Warhol's ex-muse, fashionista, and former mistress of Alain Delon, killed in a bicycle accident. Judging by the large number of regularly renewed objects that have been placed around her tombstone (flowers, wine, cigarettes, cassettes), she continues to attract admirers of both sexes.

04.

Glockenturmstraße 3
S3, 9 (Pichelsberg)

THE PARABOLIC MIRRORS OF THE 'ERSCHIESSUNGSSTÄTTE V'

A peculiarly reflective memorial to a former Nazi execution site

Between the ice rink and the Waldbühne, on the pavement on Glockenturmstraße, there is a strange traffic mirror. As it is tilted to face passers-by, it is apparently not being used for the safety of vehicles arriving at the ice rink. A short text inscribed directly onto the mirror tells us that the forest track that branches off from this point leads to the 'Erschießungsstätte V' (execution site V) in Murellenberge.

This is actually where deserters, conscientious objectors, those who had refused to obey orders and, more generally, all the 'subversive elements undermining the war effort' were executed. The names of 252 victims are known, but their number could be much greater.

Other mirrors have been placed along the track leading to the place where the execution posts are thought to have been, increasing in number as we walk down the track, forming small groups at the end of it in the middle of the forest. The texts that are engraved on 15 of the 104 mirrors relate the military past of this zone. At the end, there are extracts from witness accounts: 'I vaguely heard parts of an execution sentence being read out: Obergefreiter (chief corporal) [...] aged [...] for desertion [...] to death [...], the Maat (second-master) [...] aged [...] sentenced [...] for cowardice before the enemy [...] to be shot [...]'.

This unusual and remarkable memorial walk was devised by Patricia Pisani, an Argentinian artist living in Berlin and winner of the competition organised to design the memorial. The mirrors metaphorically reflect 'what happens at intersections when there is no visibility: a risk or potentially imminent danger that cannot yet be seen. They show something that is out of sight from the place where we are standing at the turning point, in the past, in the future.'

The death sentences pronounced by the Nazi court martial, condemning the deserters and 'saboteurs of the fighting forces' were considered, for many years, as being legitimate, and it was only in 1998 that those who had been convicted were exonerated.

The forest of Murellenberge was used by the military as early as 1840: The Royal Infantry's shooting school in Ruhleben had set up many shooting ranges and Shanzen (detached entrenchments of the fortifications). This is why the zone is called 'Schanzenwald'. A surviving example of a Schanze can be seen on the tennis court at the corner of Havelchaussee and Elsgrabenweg. In 2007, the 38-hectare plot of land that had been used for military training was cleared of its ammunition and buildings before being given back to the general public.

05.

U-Bahnmuseum (Metro Museum)
Rossitter Weg 1
U2 (Olympiastadion)

THE OLYMPIA SIGNAL BOX

The right end of the stick

Every second Saturday in the month, on the lowest level of the Olympiastadion station, visitors can gain access to more than just the tracks of the U2 metro line: U-Bahnmuseum of Berlin, housed in the old signal box of the Olympiastadion station (Olympia-Stellwerk), is also accessible here. At the end of a little corridor, you are given a 'ticket' to go to a sort of viewpoint overlooking the tracks in front of the Grunewald depot, the current command and regional control post which replaced the old signal box of the Olympia-Stellwerk in 1983.

The highlight of the visit is a technical gem, which has remained intact, and for the most part, is still in working order: the level actuators of the electromechanical signal box, type VES 1913. It started operating in 1931 and was the largest signal box of its kind in Europe. Imagine a 14-metre long keyboard, on which each note was produced by operating a lever. The partition looked like an immense optical control panel, placed just opposite, showing all the tracks of the Grunewald depot. Each engine and each signal is represented by a small light, the colour of which indicates their position at any given time.

On the wooden console, the switch operating levers are as large as those of an emergency handbrake on a vehicle, and are topped with large, blue buttons. These levers controlled 103 trains and 99 signals by managing 616 different train movement configurations. All the movements of tracks from the Grunewald depot and the metro station Olympiastadion were managed from this nerve centre, possessing the best possible view of all the rolling stock. All train movements as well as the positions of the signals and the tracks were displayed, thanks to 1,239 light bulbs, on a control panel that was six metres long and two metres high. During visits, the association AG Berliner U-Bahn, which brings together former employees of the metro, can still put on a demonstration of how this unique, electromechanical signal box was used. In an adjoining room, there is a giant relay station from which the commands from the signal box were transmitted by electrical impulses to the equipment on the tracks and the signals.

Olympia-Stadion
40
41
42
43
a/b
44
a/b
45

06.

Hohenzollerndamm 130A
S41 (Hohenzollerndamm)

KREUZKIRCHE

An expressionist masterpiece

Rare are the Berliners, and even more so the tourists, who have been inside the listed Kreuzkirche church, which is a real pity: built between 1927 and 1929, from plans drawn by Günther Paulus, it is a masterpiece of expressionist architecture.

Other than its three-pointed steeple, which can be seen from afar (54 metres high), the church has a surprising front door – in blue ceramic, reminiscent of an Asian pagoda.

On either side of the door, on the sides of the main tower, it is interesting to note the zigzag of decorations (in brick), typical of expressionist architecture. Partially rebuilt after the war in 1953, the church was renovated in 1984, respecting the original plans as faithfully as possible. Inside, a corridor leads to a remarkable main hall (octagonally-shaped) whose exceptional decor painted behind the altar is also typical of expressionism.

The original colours, created by Erich Wolde, corresponded to those of a rainbow: the entrance (*Brauthalle*) in yellow, the corridor in red, the main hall in green, the pews for the worshippers in blue (the only original colour that remains today) and the area around the altar in purple.

The harmony and architectural balance which flows from this place is definitely worth taking in for a moment on the pews of this church.

130
a
1929

07.

Hittorfstraße 5
U3 Freie Universität (Thielplatz)

RUINE DER KÜNSTE

Art inside a crumbling house

Just a few steps from the ultra-modern Philological Library at Freie Universität and nestled among stately bourgeois villas lies the Ruine der Künste (Ruins of the Arts) – a surprising venue for contemporary art housed in what appears to be a derelict home.

Above the gate, a lamp hanging from a metal arch bathes each visitor in light before they enter. A sign reads: 'The Ruine der Künste is a private space for material and immaterial arts.' It sets the tone for what's inside: the damaged façade of a 1930s villa, still visibly marked with shrapnel damage and left just as Wolf Kahlen, the current owner, found it in 1981 – abandoned after the bombings of 1945.

A conceptual artist deeply influenced by Fluxus, Kahlen had the foresight to see that the interplay between ruins and art would one day resonate. He restored only the interior, altering the original structure as little as possible, and created a nonprofit space to host both his own work and that of others.

Over the 35 years since Ruine der Künste opened its doors, more than 400 conceptual artists have been invited to show their work there – much of it created in direct response to the space itself.

On the balcony, wild grasses and weeds run riot ('a true nature reserve', as Kahlen describes it), yet a screen glimmers in the middle of the overgrowth.

Timo Kahlen, Wolf's son, is also an artist with an international presence. He lives in the former attic apartment and has made sound installations his signature medium.

A 2005 manifesto for the Ruine declares: 'Artists of the world, unite. / Find truths within yourselves. Your own, to begin with. / Everyone is the center of the world. / Seek out the skeletons of your inner values.'

RUINE DER KÜNSTE BERLI

08.

Krahmerstraße 6
S25, 26 (Lichterfelde Ost)

THE MÄUSEBUNKER

A little-known masterpiece of Brutalist architecture

Known as the Mäusebunker (the Mouse Bunker), the Research Center for Experimental Medicine (Forschungseinrichtung für experimentelle Medizin), its official name, is one of Berlin's most spectacular buildings.

A masterpiece of Brutalist architecture, this exceptional building, nearly 120 meters long and shaped like a giant warship, stands between Hindenburgdamm and Krahmerstraße, along the Teltow Canal (from which it is hidden by trees).

Although the building is no longer in use and not open to the public, you can get a good view of it from Krahmerstraße between the canal and Hindenburgdamm.

The building was designed as an animal experimentation laboratory for the Freie Universität between 1967 and 1970 by Berlin architect Gerd Hänska in collaboration with his wife Magdalena and his son Thomas. Delayed time and again, construction was not completed until 1981.

Built of concrete, the building features a striking truncated pyramid structure. The large blue tubes, resembling cannons, that protrude from both side walls give visitors the impression of standing before a warship rather than a simple research center.

These tubes once served as ventilation ducts, essential for maintaining adequate airflow within the interior spaces. The protruding triangular windows, visible on the west façade, allowed sunlight to ensure proper temperature and lighting.

09.

Platz des 4. Juli
S25, 26 (Osdorfer Straße)

4TH OF JULY SQUARE

The former '4th Ring' of the Germania project

Not far from the Teltow canal, to the west of the Lichterfeld cemetery (Städtischer Parkfriedhof Lichterfelde), a huge asphalted area suddenly becomes apparent: 460 metres long and 40 metres wide – the size of four football pitches. There is no path or barrier. This square is probably the largest asphalted piece of land in Berlin with no clearly defined purpose.

This is where, in 1994, Bill Clinton, Helmut Kohl and Eberhard Diepgen, the former mayor of Berlin, met to mark the withdrawal of the American troops who had been stationed since 1945 in the old Telefunken factory (a radio electrical company) built at the side of the square.

The American soldiers actually rehearsed marching for American national Independence Day on this large square, and this is why it was renamed 4th of July square, the day on which the USA became independent from Great Britain (4 July 1776).

Today the square is a great playground for bikers and skaters, and is also used for flea markets.

This place used to be called the '4th Ring', the name that Albert Speer gave it when he built the first part of what was supposed to become the fourth motorway ring road (the furthest from the centre) of the capital of the Reich, the future Germania (see page 112).

Hitler was always wary of plans and models and preferred to see models, even partially, at a one to one scale. Whilst visiting the Telefunken plant (with its reminder of the Electra figure at the base of the tower overlooking the square) Hitler gave his approval to the '4th Ring'.

The construction project was then shelved due to the Second World War.

The Telefunken factory buildings (which were later to house the McNair Barracks for the Americans and which today offer loft apartments to the wealthier part of the population) were built by forced labour. Where Wismarer Straße crosses the Teltow canal, a pillar-shaped concrete sculpture stands as a reminder of the labour camp barracks and in memory of the prisoners of war.

10.

Opposite Inselstraße 5
S1, 3, 7 (Nikolassee)

THE COLUMN ON SCHWANENWERDER ISLAND

Remains of the Parisian Tuileries Palace

A 15-minute walk from the beach at Wannsee, on Schwanenwerder Island (which, for a time, was nicknamed 'Bonzenwerder' after key members of the Nazi party who lived there: Goebbels, Speer, Scholtz-Klink and Morell), to the right of Inselstraße there is a tall column with a Corinthian capital standing against some ruins.

As the plaque on the column tells us, it is a small part of the original façade of the *Palais des Tuileries* (Tuileries Palace) in Paris, which was destroyed during the commune's 1871 uprising.

Hugo von Platen, who owned the island, sold it to Friedrich Wilhelm Wessel, an oil lamp manufacturer in Kreuzberg. The new owner, a speculator, true to the spirit of the *Gründerzeit*, the economic boom which began in Germany after the 1870 war, split the island up into individual plots. In order to make them more attractive for sale, he created a landscaped park bordering onto these romantic places that were greatly sought-after at the time, one of which was near the old column from the Palais de Tuileries. He also lived to see his island officially renamed Schwanenwerder (Swan Island) by imperial decree in 1901.

In the background, there is an inscription above the bench which is opposite the Havel, reminding us of the transitory nature of happiness: 'This stone from the banks of the Seine / transplanted to the land of the Germans, / Warns you, the passer-by: / Oh happiness, how fickle you are!'

This entreaty must have been an oracle not only for Wessel but also for all the other inhabitants of the island. After the war and the departure of the Nazis, the column narrowly escaped being dismantled and taken back to Paris: the French suspected the Germans of having stolen the remains of Tuileries Palace during the 1871 military campaign, and considered them to be the Prussians' perfidious spoils of war.

By collecting all existing evidence, it was possible to prove to the French that the fragments of the columns and other elements from the façade of the Tuileries Palace had, in fact, all been legally acquired by Wessel. They had even been put up for sale to the public in 1882 in Paris as decorative architectural elements.

© Adobe Stock / Achim Wagner

11.

Pfaueninsel (Peacock Island)
S7 Potsdam Hauptbahnhof then bus 218 (Wannsee Bhf.)

THE COMMEMORATIVE STONE AT THE KUNCKEL GLASSWORKS

The Alchemist's Legend

At the far northern tip of Berlin's Peacock Island, just a few hundred metres from the Beelitz hunting lodge, a commemorative stone marks the site of the long-lost Kunckel glassworks, destroyed by fire. Legend has it that the blaze was set by rivals shortly after the death of Kunckel's patron, Frederick William of Brandenburg. The stone reads: 'Johann Kunckel built his laboratory on this island in 1685. He produced phosphorus and ruby glass here.'

Born around 1635, Johann Kunckel was trained in chemistry and pharmacy and eventually summoned to the court in Dresden by John George II, Elector of Saxony, who awarded him a generous salary as a goldsmith and alchemist.

However, his attempts at transmutation failed, and when Elector of Saxony refused to continue paying him, Kunckel was forced to find new employment.

In 1677, the personal physician of the Great Elector Frederick William invited him to the Brandenburg court. Officially, his mission was to replenish state coffers by turning base metals into gold and silver – but the Elector had more pragmatic plans.

After the devastation of the Thirty Years' War, Brandenburg was impoverished, and Frederick William hoped to revitalise the region through the production of high-quality glass using local quartz.

Kunckel began experimenting in 1678 at the Drewitz

Examples of Kunckel's ruby glass and a first edition of his treatise *Ars Vitraria Experimentalis* (*The Perfect Art of Glassmaking*) can be seen at the Potsdam Museum (Am Alten Markt 9).

A street in Babelsberg is named in his honour – Johann-Kunckel-Strasse – where he also had a workshop. In 2005, archaeologists uncovered fragments of coloured glass during construction works on Friedrich-Engels-Strasse near the Nuthe bridge. These are thought to be remnants from his original glassworks.

glassworks, and the following year he launched a second workshop on the Hakendamm (now roughly Friedrich-Engels-Strasse). The venture was a success, with historic records indicating an annual production of 30,000 to 50,000 pieces.

Then in 1684, Kunckel achieved a breakthrough: he rediscovered the lost technique for producing 'ruby glass', a deep red variety made by adding gold chloride to molten glass. Although the process was known in ancient Rome, it had been forgotten for over a millennium. Brandenburg now held a highly prized secret. Frederick William was so pleased that he granted Kunckel a lucrative monopoly on ruby glass production and, in 1685, gave him the entire island of Pfaueninsel (then called Kaninchenwerder) to continue his work. Kunckel was also granted the right to distil spirits on the island.

The smoke and odours from his furnaces, combined with the strict prohibition against anyone other than the Elector setting foot on the island, gave rise to rumours that the 'wizard of the island' was secretly practising magic and alchemical transmutation.

ALCHEMY AND PEACOCK ISLAND

In 1792, King Frederick William II acquired Pfaueninsel as an extension of the Neuer Garten, after plans to incorporate the Pfingstberg into the garden failed. As a young man, he had rowed to the island with his lover Wilhelmine Enke to read to her in secret among the reeds. On the island, the alchemist Johann Kunckel conducted secret experiments in the 17th century. Though he never discovered the philosopher's stone, he did succeed in developing the technique for making gold ruby glass (see p. 234). It's no coincidence that King Frederick William II later introduced peacocks to the island, which only then acquired its current name. The brilliantly coloured, train-like tail feathers of male peacocks – especially when fanned out in full splendour – symbolise a key phase in the alchemical process. The peacock's tail displays every colour of the rainbow, formed when white light is split through a prism. In alchemical thought, this represents the transition from *nigredo* (blackening) to *albedo* (whitening), the second major stage in the alchemical transformation.

PEACOCK IMAGERY IN THE NEUER GARTEN

You'll find peacock motifs throughout the Neuer Garten – on the ceiling of the Marble Palace's ground floor ceremonial room, for example, and on the ceiling of the shell grotto, fragments of which still remain today.

12.

Glienicke Palace
Königstraße 36
S1, 7 (Wannsee) then bus 316 (Glienicker Lake)

THE TELAMONS OF GLIENICKE PARK

They would be called corpses, wouldn't they?

In the very heart of the grounds of Glienicke Palace, to the right of the restaurant, at the base of a column near the orangery, facing north, there is what would appear from behind to be merely a pile of stones. However, a walk round the trees will reveal astonishing sculptures of men lying partially concealed in the undergrowth. Take a closer look and you will see the men from the waist up, lying on the ground, yet seemingly still holding something above their heads.

In 1863 Berlin gave these sculptures as a gift to prince Carl of Prussia (1801–1883), the owner and designer of Glienicke Palace and park. He was widely known to be an avid collector: it was common knowledge that he sent for whole sections of monasteries which had been knocked down in Italy to be used in Glienicke Palace on the Havel. He collected everything as long as it was in some way an antiquity: fragments of reliefs, mosaic floors, mural decorations, capitals, sculpted pieces and fragments of balustrades. They were torn from their original settings due to war, decline, volcanic eruptions, or even more banal reasons such as theft. This is how the charmingly named pavilion, *Kleine Neugierde* (Little Curiosity) in Glienicke park, came to be fitted with a mosaic floor from Ancient Carthage.

Prince Carl, however, was not sure what to do with the gift from Berlin: four legless telamons from the Palace am Festungsgraben (near the moat of the fortifications), the residence of Johann Gottfried Donner, who was the personal valet of Frederick II and Elisabeth of Prussia, his estranged wife. The frontage of his palace had been built some hundred years before in the 'Hellenistic' Renaissance style. From 1808 onwards, the palace then served as a workplace for 48 finance ministers. The telamons were sculpted in Silesian sandstone from the drawings of a sculptor and porcelain artist, Ernst Heinrich Reichard (died in 1764) who made the KPM royal porcelain factory famous. They still lie here, waiting to go to another place one day. Who knows?

13.

Königstraße
S1/S7 Wannsee then bus 316 (Schloss Glienicke)

THE REMAINS OF LITTLE SWITZERLAND

High up on the mountain, there was once a little chalet ...

In Berlin, no mountains. A few round-topped hills. Nothing else. So hearing people talk about a 'Switzerland' is rather intriguing. Even more so if the place in question is really a steep slope.

Home to the Loggia Alexandra, the mountain of Böttcherberg (66 m) is an exception as it is not a man-made hill, made, as many hills are in Berlin, of rubble from ruins from the war. It was formed naturally and dates back to the Ice Age. This explains why many boulders, the remains of an old glacier, can be seen scattered among ancient oaks.

From 1841, Prince Carl of Prussia had this miniature wilderness made into an alpine rock garden – a 'Switzerland' as it was called in those days. As a prelude to this, a mini navigable canal was dug in the valley (the Bäkenkanal) and 'Swiss' chalets were built on the slope facing Potsdam, some of which are still standing today. A small mountain cemetery and a chapel (still standing) lined the road leading to the castle of Klein-Glienicke. This road began with a climb up to an alpine glade, where hikers and walkers could get something to eat and quench their thirst with a glass of milk or beer, before starting the real 'climb'.

Remnants of former clay extraction activities meant that there was a trench that had been dug here, making it easy to create an alpine Switzerland: the beginning of a narrow mule track was scattered with artificial rock needles and plants from the rock garden. The track led up to the summit of Böttcherberg.

There was also a hillside vine with steps carved into the rock, all contributing to the impression of being at the foot of a mountain.

At that time, this type of landscape architecture, which was created with a good deal of concrete mortar, bricks and limestone from Rüdersdorf, was the first of its kind in Prussia.

The rocky outcrops can still be seen, in addition to the high walls that were built for vine growing.

14.

Königstraße
S1/S7 (Wannsee) then bus 316 (Schloss Glienicke)

THE HELICOPTER OF STEINSTÜCKEN

Steinstücken, an enclave of West Berlin in the GDR, with its own wall

It is hard to imagine a more unusual monument: rotor blades from helicopters from the 1960s belonging to the American Army, standing upright like a rifle that you would carry on your shoulder, on the edge of a children's playground ... There is, in fact, a helicopter in the playground: it is made of colourful tubes welded together, and is used as a climbing frame, much to the children's delight, as if helicopters were something special here.

Between 1961 and 1972, American military helicopters did in fact land and take off here, every day, to supply Steinstücken, an enclave of West Berlin in the heart of the GDR, with basic provisions (see page 246). At that time, the tiny enclave of Steinstücken had a population of around 300 inhabitants and was part of the Wannsee district (Bezirk Steglitz-Zehlendorf), even although it was located in the very centre of Potsdam-Neubabelsberg. In 1920 when Greater Berlin was created, this village had already found itself 'out on a limb', but, at first, it had not really mattered to the inhabitants who felt attached to Babelsberg. However, between 1945 and 1971, things were to take an unexpected turn. In October 1951, the GDR failed to annex Steinstücken when, after four days of occupation, the Americans intervened and freed the enclave. In 1952, the GDR fenced it in. For the inhabitants who numbered no more than 200 people at the time, there was only one possible road left that they could take to get to Wannsee, and it was controlled by the GDR. Visitors and suppliers had to prove that they had a holiday home in Steinstücken. After the wall was built in 1961, three American soldiers remained stationed in Steinstücken and, from that time onwards, helicopters helped out with supplies. However, the GDR was supplying Steinstücken with electricity and water. After the Quadripartite Agreement on Berlin was concluded in 1971, which stated that the 'problems of enclaves, including that of Steinstücken, and of other areas of land, can be solved by exchanges of land', Steinstücken was linked to Wannsee by an umbilical cord that was 900 metres long and 100 metres wide. The GDR having relocated the walls, a large road, coming to a dead end, was inaugurated on 30 August 1972 by the mayor of Berlin, Klaus Schütz, which enabled the village to be connected to public transport (Bus 118). From then on, West Berlin could also supply the village with electricity and water. As the helicopters had stopped flying backwards and forwards, the children got bored. Their parents, however, were delighted to see the price of their land soar and to at last be able to park in front of their houses. When tourists began flooding to Berlin, some of the inhabitants, who had enjoyed both the heroic and comical side of their insularity, started missing the past. But, since then, everything seems to have come to a happy end.

© OTFW

15.

Kanalauenweg
Bus 628 (Kleinmachnow, Lindenbahn) / S7 (Griebnitzsee) then bus 628 (Stolper Weg)

THE FORMER CHECKPOINT OF DREILINDEN

The unfortunate route of the former motorway

When looking at the bridge over the Teltow canal from the south, it seems obvious that this derelict construction, which would at first appear to be rather ordinary, is in fact anything but that. On this large bridge, the worn-out asphalt of which is overgrown with trees, white marks indicate the tracks reserved for various categories of vehicle – busses, PKW (cars) and LKW (heavy goods vehicles). The motorway actually used to run through the forest which was an extremely popular place with Berlin's biggest archery club, which practises further down the way.

At the end of the Second World War, the bridge crossed not only the canal but also the border which had just been drawn between the East and the West. (A little piece of West Berlin, Teerofen attached to Wannsee, jutted out into GDR territory and the exact point where the border with the GDR crossed the canal lay directly under the bridge.) The identity of the people travelling between the GDR and West Berlin had already been checked at the Drewitz GÜST, the border control of the GDR. It is for this reason that the first Allied checkpoints, and those of West Berlin's police and customs, were set up on the bridge to check the vehicles travelling to West Berlin. Premises were built to watch over the border crossings from the south bank of the canal. In front of it, flag staffs were placed on either side: (to the south) there were American, British and French flags, and (to the north), the flags of the GDR and West Berlin. The, now flagless, poles are still there today.

However, after the checkpoint of Dreilinden, the journey continued for about three kilometres into the GDR, before crossing the border a second time to get into West Berlin, just before the motorway interchange of Zehlendorfer Kreuz. In 1969, in order to get round the western appendix jutting into its territory (and the problems caused by the infamous three kilometres), the GDR modified this route. The border controls were subsequently carried out just before the Zehlendorf interchange, whilst keeping the old names (Drewitz/Dreilinden/Checkpoint Bravo) intact. Today, the Checkpoint Bravo association ensures the upkeep of the memorial in the former watchtower of the border control (GÜST) of the GDR, situated in the municipality of Stahnsdorf.

Slightly to the north of the former border control of Dreilinden, a few minutes away on foot, the old route of the motorway can be clearly seen from a bridge, giving a good idea of where the motorway actually ran.

THE EXTRAORDINARY HISTORY OF BERLIN'S EXCLAVES

Today's Berlin is the consequence of the creation of Greater Berlin on 1 October 1920, which brought together around a hundred towns, villages and territories surrounding the old Berlin, leading to the creation of a dozen exclaves which were enclaved in the heart of the neighbouring province of Brandenburg. In 1945, with the occupation of Germany after the Second World War, the former exclaves of Berlin, dependent on the American and British zones, thus became the exclaves of the Soviet zone, and then from 1949, those of East Germany.

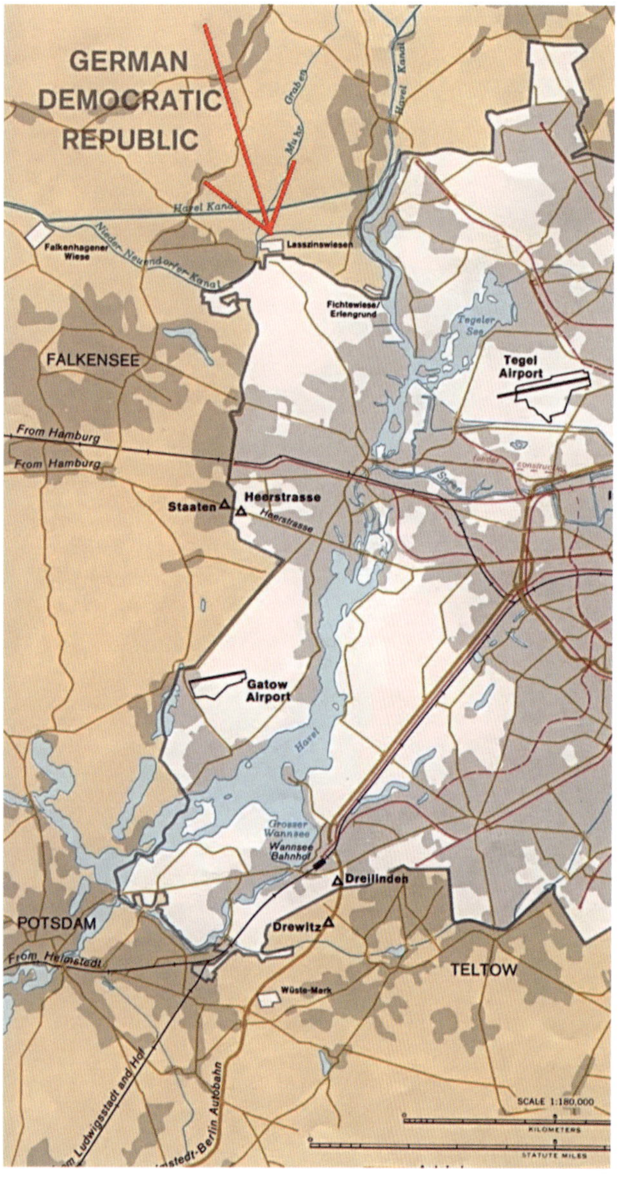

The existence of these exclaves was inevitably the cause of much tension, notably in Steinstücken, the only inhabited exclave.

To make travelling between West Berlin and its exclaves easier, three agreements were signed:

- On 21 December 1971, an agreement was made to abolish six exclaves in exchange for territories: East Germany received the exclaves of Böttcherberg, Fichtenwiesen, Große Kuhlake and Nuthewiesen (15.6 ha in total) from West Berlin, in exchange for 17.1 ha: the question of Steinstücken was resolved by attaching the village of West Berlin by a strip of land. West Berlin had to pay 4 million marks to East Germany for this extra territory (2.3 ha).
- On 21 July 1972, East Germany sold 8.5 hectares of land which had previously belonged to Mitte, corresponding to the old station of Potsdamer Platz, for 31million marks.
- On 31 March 1988, a final exchange was made in order to (amongst other things) abolish the last five remaining exclaves: East Germany received Falkenhagener Wiese, Finkenkrug and Wüste Mark in addition to a 50-metre long strip of land running along the front of the goods station of Eberswalder, to the north of Bernauer Strasse (Wedding), which is part of the Mauerpark today (for a total of 87.3 ha). West Berlin was allowed to add Erlengrund and Fichtenwiesen to its territory and it also retreived 14 territories along the border, as well as the Lenné-Dreieck (a triangular-shaped territory near Potsdamer Platz) for 76 million marks (96.7 ha in total). In this way, West Berlin expanded its territory by 9.4 ha with, in particular, the territory of Tiefwerder, East Berlin's former exclave of the west (Spandau), which officially became a territory of Spandau (West Berlin).

WEST BERLIN'S 12 EXCLAVES IN THE EAST WERE AS FOLLOWS:

- Böttcherberg (0.30 ha): three distinct, uninhabited strips of land ranging from 20 to 100 metres long by a few metres in width, very close to Berlin's south-west border near Königstraße. Given up to East Germany in 1971, they are now part of Potsdam.
- Erlengrund (0.51 ha) and Fichtenwiesen (3.51 ha): two plots of land near Berlin, just north of the Spandauer Forst, near the Havel. These two plots were maintained by West Berlin's gardening associations: to get there, members had to go through a gate in the Berlin Wall, walk down a path, escorted by East German border guards, and then go through a checkpoint. This access, which was reserved for members of the associations, was only possible at certain times. The path in East German territory was fenced in on either side to block access from East Germany. The two enclaves were eliminated in 1988 when East Germany gave up the surrounding land to West Berlin.
- Falkenhagener Wiese (45.44 ha): the largest and furthest of the enclaves, 5 km from West Berlin's borders. This derelict land was given up to East Germany in 1988 and is now part of Falkensee.
- Finkenkrug (3.45 ha): a derelict plot of land, 5 km west of Berlin, was given up to East Germany in 1971 and is now part of Falkensee.
- Große Kuhlake (8.03 ha): a derelict plot of land near Berlin's border, was given up to East Germany in 1971 and is now part of Falkensee.
- Laszinswiesen (13.49 ha): a derelict plot situated immediately north of Berlin's border, given up to East Germany in 1988 and which is now part Schönwalde.
- Nuthewiesen (3.64 ha): an uninhabited marshland area, given up to East Germany in 1971 and which is now part of Potsdam.

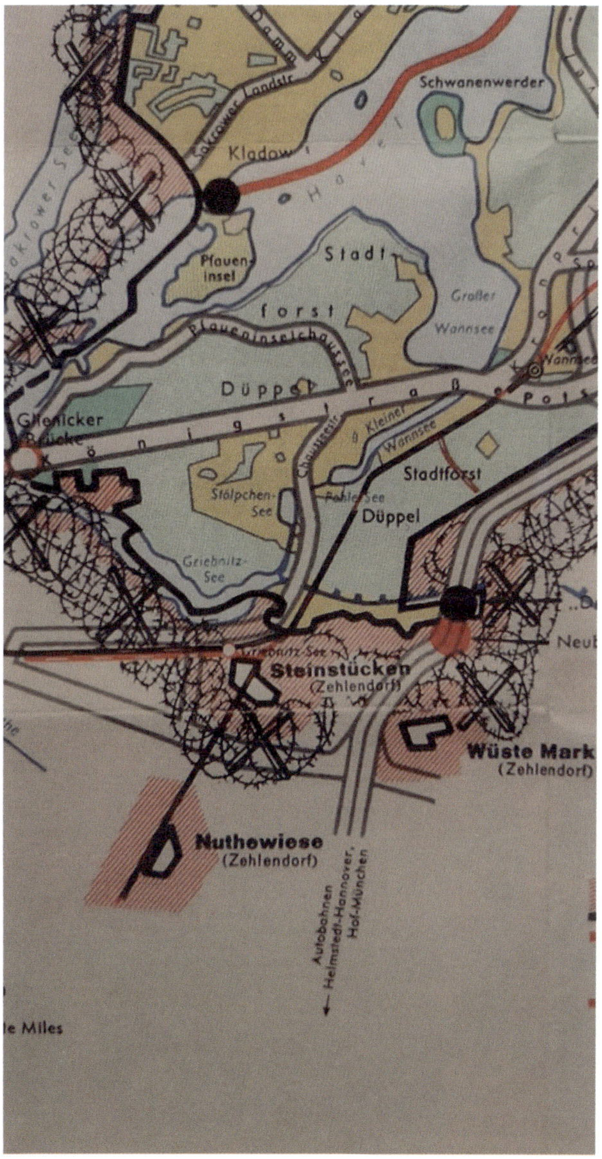

- Steinstücken (12. 67 ha): The only inhabited west German enclave (see page 242).
- Wüste Mark (21. 83 ha): given up to East Germany in 1988, it is now part of Stahnsdorf.

16.

South-West Cemetery of Stahnsdorf (Südwestkirchhof Stahnsdorf)
Bahnhofstraße 2, 14532 Stahnsdorf
Bus X1 from Potsdam Central Station to Stahnsdorf (Meisenweg)

THE TOMB OF JULIUS WISSINGER

An expressionist masterpiece by Max Taut

Just a hundred metres south of the cemetery chapel in Stahnsdorf, nestled in the shade of a striking and unconventional funerary monument, lies the final resting place of the Wissinger family. The tomb was designed by Berlin architect Max Taut and constructed between 1922 and 1923. Its design echoes the skeletal frame of a Gothic nave, with eight pillars supporting ten pointed arches. These vaulted spans, formed from reinforced concrete, divide the structure into three bays, each housing gravestones.

This unique piece was created while Max Taut was active in the artistic circle known as the *Gläserne Kette* ('Glass Chain'), a visionary group of architects who, in 1919–1920, dreamed of a new, transparent, dynamic architecture – a so-called 'architecture of glass.' Though most of the designs from this period remained unrealised, the Wissinger family tomb stands as the group's only significant architectural legacy brought to life. Taut received the commission from Julius Wissinger (1884–1965), a patron of the arts, and his wife Helene, following the death of Julius's father in 1920.

The Wissinger family rose to affluence in the late 19th century through their successful grain and seed trade. Their former warehouse, a finely restored example of industrial architecture, can still be seen at Pfuelstraße 5–8, along the banks of the River Spree in Berlin.

The Gläserne Kette was founded by Max's brother, Bruno Taut, and consisted primarily of architects who exchanged ideas and projects by post. The group was instrumental in shaping German Expressionism – an artistic and philosophical movement rooted in the existential realisation that 'God is dead,' as Nietzsche proclaimed, that transcendence is an illusion, and that the soul is fundamentally material. This philosophical thread runs through the monument designed by Max Taut: a sacred space (the tomb) emerges from inert matter (volcanic rock enclosing the grave). In line with this materialist theme, a sculpture originally included with the tomb – by artist Otto Freundlich – depicted a golem: a mythical being of clay brought to life by its maker, yet still nothing more than living matter.

It was September 1995 and Thomas Jonglez was in Peshawar, the northern Pakistani city, 20 kilometres from the tribal zone he was to visit a few days later. It occurred to him that he should record the hidden aspects of his native city, Paris, which he knew so well. During his seven-month trip back home from Beijing, the countries he crossed included Iran and Kurdistan. He never took a plane but travelled by boat, train or bus, hitchhiking, cycling, on horseback or on foot, reaching Paris just in time to celebrate Christmas with the family.

On his return, he spent two fantastic years wandering the streets of the capital to gather material for his first "secret guide", written with a friend. For the next seven years he worked in the steel industry until the passion for discovery overtook him. He launched Jonglez Publishing in 2003 and moved to Venice three years later.

In 2013, in search of new adventures, the family left Venice and spent six months travelling to Brazil, via North Korea, Micronesia, the Solomon Islands, Easter Island, Peru and Bolivia.

After seven years in Rio de Janeiro, he now lives in Berlin with his wife and three children.

Jonglez Publishing produces a range of titles in nine languages, released in 40 countries.

Atlas of curiosities

Atlas of abandoned France
Atlas of extreme weather
Atlas of forbidden places
Atlas of geographical curiosities
Atlas of geographical curiosities - Britain
Atlas of unusual wines
Atlas of urban vineyards

Secret Atlas

Berlin - The secret atlas
London - The secret atlas
New York - The secret atlas
Paris - The secret atlas
Rome - The secret atlas
Venice - The secret atlas

'Soul of' guides

Soul of Amsterdam
Soul of Athens
Soul of Barcelona
Soul of Berlin
Soul of Brussels
Soul of Detroit
Soul of Kyoto
Soul of Lisbon
Soul of Los Angeles
Soul of Marrakesh
Soul of Marseille
Soul of Milan
Soul of New York
Soul of Paris
Soul of Rome
Soul of Tokyo
Soul of Venice
Soul of Vienna

Photo books

Abandoned America
Abandoned Asylums
Abandoned Australia
Abandoned Belgium
Abandoned Churches: Unclaimed places of worship
Abandoned cinemas of the world
Abandoned France
Abandoned Germany
Abandoned Italy
Abandoned Japan
Abandoned Lebanon
Abandoned Spain
Abandoned USSR
Abandoned world – An AI-generated exploration
After the Final Curtain – The Fall of the American Movie Theater
After the Final Curtain – America's Abandoned Theaters
Baikonur – Vestiges of the Soviet space programme
Cinemas – A French heritage
Clickbait – A visual journey through AI-generated stories
Forbidden France
Forbidden Places – Vol. 1
Forbidden Places – Vol. 2
Forbidden Places – Vol. 3
Forgotten France
Forgotten Heritage
Oblivion
Parisian Theatres
Secret sacred sites
Venice deserted
Venice from the skies

'Secret' guides

Secret Amsterdam
Secret Bali – An unusual guide
Secret Bangkok
Secret Barcelona
Secret Bath – An unusual guide
Secret Belfast
Secret Berlin
Secret Boston – An unusual guide
Secret Brighton – An unusual guide
Secret Brooklyn – An unusual guide
Secret Brussels
Secret Budapest
Secret Buenos Aires
Secret Campania
Secret Cape Town
Secret Copenhagen
Secret Corsica
Secret Dolomites
Secret Dublin – An unusual guide
Secret Edinburgh – An unusual guide
Secret Florence
Secret French Riviera
Secret Geneva
Secret Glasgow
Secret Granada
Secret Helsinki
Secret Istanbul
Secret Johannesburg
Secret Kuala Lumpur
Secret Lisbon
Secret Liverpool – An unusual guide
Secret London – An unusual guide
Secret London – Unusual bars & restaurants
Secret Los Angeles – An unusual guide
Secret Louisiana – An unusual guide
Secret Madrid
Secret Mexico City
Secret Milan
Secret Montreal – An unusual guide
Secret Naples
Secret New Orleans – An unusual guide
Secret New York – An unusual guide
Secret New York – Curious activities
Secret New York – Hidden bars & restaurants
Secret Normandy
Secret Paris
Secret Potsdam
Secret Prague
Secret Provence
Secret Rio de Janeiro
Secret Rome
Secret Seville
Secret Singapore
Secret Stockholm
Secret Strasbourg
Secret Sussex – An unusual guide
Secret Tokyo
Secret Tuscany
Secret Venice
Secret Venice Lagoon
Secret Vienna
Secret Washington D.C. – An unusual guide
Secret York – An unusual guide

Follow us on Facebook and Instagram

ACKNOWLEDGEMENTS

Andy Altmeier, Paula Anke, Nicholas Bamberger, Mathilde Bonbon, Élodie Bouchereau, Veronika Kellndorfer, Karim Ben Khalifa, Constance Breton, Ekaterina Emchenko, Oliver Euchner, Uwe Fabich, Bodo Förster, Michael Fuchs, Daniel Heer, Jan Kleihues, Michaela Lindinger, Frédéric Lucas, Elizabeth Markevitch, Daniele Maruca, Amélie de Maupeou, Delphine Mousseau, Suraj Nathwany, Pascale Nicoulaud, Mathilde Ramadier, Bertrand Saint-Guilhem, Philipp Schüneman, Carsten Seiler, Tommy Spree, Patrick Suel, Dr Georg Thaler, Hemma Thaler, Anja Weber, Lilith Zink.

Manuel Roy:
I would like to give my hearfelt thanks to those who so generously supported and accompanied me during my research and explorations of Berlin: my friends Gerhard Schwarz and Sunhwa Lee, Mrs Sandra Rohwedder from the German Foundation for the Protection of Historic Monuments (Deutsche Stiftung Denkmalschutz), Mr Hans Riefel from the Regional Office of Historic Monuments (Landesdenkmalamt), Mr Jörg Kuhn from the Berlin Mitte Evangelist Cemeteries Association, Mrs Annette Winkelmann from the Carl-Gotthard-Langhas Society, Mrs Isabella Mannozzi from the Bildgießerei Noak, Mr Yeter Hanefi, as well as the many anonymous Berliners I met at the various places I investigated who so joyfully shared their often astonishing wealth of knowledge. *Berlin, ick liebe dir.*

PHOTOGRAPHY CREDITS

Photographs by **Tom Wolf**:
Rabbit silhouettes on Chausseestraße – Windows of the Invalids' House – Stone of Monbijou Park – Handshake on Sophienstraße – Honi's window – Dolphin sculpture – Crypt of the Parochialkirche – Wusterhausischer Bär – Toll wall – Underground house – Toad at the Prinzenstraße underground station – Visit to the Malzfabrik (top photo) – Alfred Hrdlicka's 'Danse macabre' – Binninger's clock – Wedding sand dune – Spa pavilion bas–relief – Stairs of the ULAP – Kerbs of Germania – Gas street lamps of the open air museum – Visit to the UT2 – Cherubs of Pankow – Grunewald forest cemetery – Olympia signal box – 4th of July square – Helicopter of Steinstücken

Photographs by **Manuel Roy**:
Façade of Thomasiusstraße 5

Photographs by **Roberto Sassi**:
James Turrell lighting installation – Water tanks of Prenzlauer Berg

Photographs by **Bertrand Saint-Guilhem**:
Hall of the Moabit Courthouse – Entrance gates of the Ceciliengärten – Tomb of Julius Wissinger

Photographs by **Thomas Jonglez**:
Animal anatomical theatre – Staircase of the Max Delbrück Center – White cross of Saint Mary's Church – Remains of the city walls (up photo) – Geschäftshaus Tietz – Ermeler House bas–reliefs – Historical milestone on Dönhoff Platz – Alfandary House bas–reliefs – Staircase of the German Steelworkers Union – Remains of the Stresemannstraße railway line – Grave of the Mühlenhaupt family – Oppenfeld family mausoleum – Tomb of Erwin Reibedanz – Stehfisch sculpture – Reliefs on the facade of Adalbertstraße 79 – Theodor Fontane's pharmacy – Two-wheeler Museum – Art installations on Reichenberger Straße – Forgotten symbols of the Ideal–Passage – Stones of Alfred–Scholz–Platz – Café Botanico garden – Sri Mayurapathy Murugan Hindu temple – Windows of the Church of the Twelve Apostles – Mosaic of a cow – Orte des Erinnerns memorial – Visit to the Malzfabrik (bottom photo) – Natur–Park–Südgelände – House at Niedstraße 4 – Eisack tunnel – Monument to the glory of motorcycle racers – Stained–glass windows of the Church on the Hohenzollernplatz – Hall of the Moabit Courthouse – Paper leaves of the Swiss Embassy – Well in the Jewish cemetery – Coat of arms of the Grüne Stadt Gate – Tomb of the Lewinsohn et Netter

families – Columns of Weberwiese – Geological Wall – Painter of the Motorwerk – Trudelturm vertical wind tunnel – Schmetterlingshorst butterfly collection – Isothermal spherical laboratories – Staakens's old control tower – The fields of Karolinenhöhe – The parabolic mirrors of the 'Erschiessungsstätte V' – A104 motorway tunnel building – Lahore Ahmadiyya Movement Mosque – Red letterbox in Fehrbelliner Platz – Kreuzkirche – Mäusebunker – The former checkpoint of Dreilinden – Remains of little Switzerland – Telamons of Glienicke park – Gertrude's mouse

Photograph by **Ansgar Koreng:** Foyer of the Berlin Courthouse (p. 40–41)

Photographs by **Dieter Brügmann**: Schwerbelastungskörper (top photo)

Photograph by **Furfur**: Schwerbelastungskörper (bottom photo)

Photograph by **Marek Sliwecki**: Michaelsen Palace

Photograph by **Jörg Zägel:** Façade of the Bethanie (top photo)

Photograph by **Sailko**: Façade of the Bethanie (bottom photo)

Photograph by **OTFW**: Johann Jacob Baeyer memorial (left page)

Photograph by **Agadez**: Johann Jacob Baeyer memorial (right page)

Photograph by **Berit Ruge**: Commemorative stone at the Kunckel glassworks

Cover photo: © Kai Nachtigal - Unsplash

Maps: **Cyrille Suss** – Layout: **Emmanuelle Willard Toulemonde** – Translation: **Ordentop and Jane Bonin** – Editing: **Matt Gay and Sigrid Newman** – Proofreading: **Abigail Kafka** – Publishing: **Clémence Mathé**

Registration of copyright: September 2026 – Edition: 01
ISBN: 978-2-36195-968-5
Printed in China by Toppan

MIX
Paper | Supporting responsible forestry
FSC® C104723